Discrimination

COPING WITH

Discrimination

Gabrielle I. Edwards

THE ROSEN PUBLISHING GROUP, INC./NEW YORK

Published in 1986, 1992 by The Rosen Publishing Group, Inc.
29 East 21st Street, New York, NY 10010

Revised Edition

Library of Congress Cataloging in Publication Data

Edwards, Gabrielle I.
    Coping with discrimination.

    (Coping)
    Bibliography: p. 134.
    Includes index.
    Summary: Examines the historical patterns and results of prejudice
and discrimination and their effects on such minorities as the homeless,
blacks, women, homosexuals, and the handicapped.
    1. Civil rights—Juvenile literature.   2. Discrimination—Juvenile
literature.   3. Prejudices—Juvenile literature.   4. Minorities—
Juvenile literature.
    [1. Discrimination.   2. Prejudices.   3. Minorities]
    I. Title.   II. Series.
    JC585.E32   1986   323.4   86-6727

    ISBN 0-8239-1426-7

Manufactured in the United States of America

This book is dedicated with love to my mother, Margaret P. Curlin, who always sought for her children the best that life could offer

Acknowledgments

I express appreciation for the help given me by: Francis D. Edwards, Frank D. Edwards, and the Southern Law Poverty Center for contributing to my research file; Charles Johnson and Marion Curlin for giving me interview time during which matters pertaining to the public and discrimination were discussed;

The Rev. Paul E.C. Hamilton, who read portions of the manuscript and offered valuable suggestions;

Moira Joseph for providing a much needed photograph;

Bill Stanton of Klanwatch, the Schomburg Collection of the New York Public Library, the International Ladies Garment Workers Union, the National Foundation–March of Dimes, the Association on American Indian Affairs, and Student Struggle for Soviet Jewry for providing photographs for this book.

G.I.E.

ABOUT THE AUTHOR ◇

Mrs. Gabrielle I. Edwards was formerly Assistant Principal Supervision of the Science Department at Franklin D. Roosevelt High School in Brooklyn. Although her areas of specialty were the biological sciences and general science, she supervised chemistry, physics, earth science, and psychobiology.

The holder of bachelor's and master's degrees in biology, general science, and education from Brooklyn College, Mrs. Edwards taught for thirty-eight years in the school system of the City of New York. After serving as a teacher of general science for four years, she was appointed to the senior high school, where she remained for thirty-four years. For twenty-three years she was the supervisor of a large and active science department.

Gabrielle Edwards is the author of several books for students in junior and senior high school, including *Coping with Drug Abuse, Coping with Discrimination, Biology the Easy Way, Laboratory Techniques for High Schools, How to Pass the Examination in Advanced Placement Biology, and Living Things* (co-authored).

Her professional affiliations include membership in the Biology Chairmen's Association, the New York Biology Teachers' Association, the Science Council of New York, the National Association of Biology Teachers, the National Science Teachers Association, the New York Academy of Science, and the Brooklyn College Alumni Association.

Because of her numerous contributions to education, Mrs. Edwards was the recipient of four prestigious honors. The first was an award presented by the President of Long Island University for her contributions to science education. The second was an award by the Board of Education of the City of New York in recognition of her outstanding performance in supervision. The third was her selection by the National Science Teachers Association as the Outstanding Science Supervisor of the Nation. The fourth award was made by the Division of Curriculum and Instruction of the New York City Board of Education for outstanding contributions to science curricula.

Although retired from the school system, Gabrielle Edwards maintains professional activity in education. She serves on the New York State Commission for Equity in Science and Math for Women and Minorities. She is also the Executive Director of St. Mary's Community Services, Inc., a nonsectarian outreach organization that prepares educational programs in the prevention of substance abuse for teenagers and young adults.

Contents

Preface

Discriminatory practices seem to be a failing of all human societies. To gain economic advantage or political power, one group sets up restrictive laws against another group. The effect of the discriminatory laws is to weaken racial, religious, or ethnic groups so that they function only minimally.

History and experience have shown us that laws that require the separation of people and prevent one or more groups in a society from achieving their potential hurt the entire society. Currently, the blacks in South Africa are going through a violent struggle to obtain their human rights. Governments the world over recognize that the government of South Africa cannot perpetuate the system of apartheid. It is an archaic model of subjugation that conflicts with modern philosophy, which stresses observance of human rights.

Coping with Discrimination by no means exhausts the subject of discrimination. Its purpose is to explore the weaknesses in society that are caused by prejudice and discrimination. The book is a prejudice sampler that begins with a thumbnail sketch of some historical patterns of prejudice and shows how they impinge on today's societies. Suggestions for change are offered through the legal systems of countries in which discriminatory laws and practices separate a part of the population from the mainstream. The book touches on modes of discrimination that affect racial groups, ethnic populations, women,

PREFACE

homosexuals, and the handicapped. People of all kinds
make up society and contribute to its culture, its inven-
tions, and its progress. The contributions of all people are
needed to make this world a better place in which to live.

Gabrielle I. Edwards

CHAPTER ◇ 1

Historical Patterns

of Discrimination

Discrimination hurts people. Discrimination is the continuous process of depriving a group of persons of their right to function fully in the community in which they live. Discrimination is the total process of isolating a group of humans, selected for some readily identifiable characteristic, and forcing them to live at the ragged edges of society barred from the mainstream of life. Discrimination separates a person from his fellow beings in a way that is demeaning. It destroys feelings of self-worth.

Discrimination also injures the discriminator, who must become adapted to a life system of hatred and prejudice. The overriding emotion of the discriminator's life must be a corrosive hostility. The laws and practices that enforce discrimination require the denial of human rights, demand separation of people, and support episodes of physical violence directed against a segment of the human population.

Discrimination and the Law

Discrimination begins with the philosophy that one group is superior to another in inherited characteristics, intelligence, work habits, and overall patterns of behavior. The dominant group strengthens this philosophy of racial, religious, or ethnic superiority by enacting laws that make it "right" to deny others their just share of life. Laws that support discrimination damage the psyche of the mainstream society, calling forth chronic feelings of ill will. Acts of hostility resulting in violence are directed against the minority group. The majority and minority groups live always at the edge of fear.

It must be recognized that legal statutes do affect the thought processes and behavior of the population at large. A recent and painful example of the effect of laws on the thinking of a population is the chain of events that took place in the United States. A system of "Jim Crow" laws dominated the very fabric of society in the thirteen Southern states, denying basic human rights to black Americans who lived in or even passed through those states. The laws mandated segregation of blacks from whites in all places of public accommodation. Black citizens of the United States had to sit in the back of the bus, drink from water fountains marked "Colored only," attend segregated schools; they were denied access to jobs and to dignity. The Civil Rights Act of 1964 made laws of segregation in places of public accommodation illegal.

The Irish Catholic Majority vs. the English Minority

Most laws that legalize discrimination are rooted in the political foundations of a society. It can happen that the dominant group of a society is not its majority group. Thus

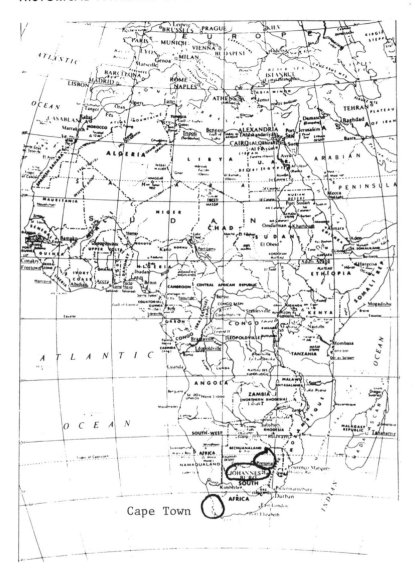

Fig. 1.1 The circled areas indicate the regions where violent protests against apartheid are taking place in South Africa.

laws are made to keep the majority (but politically weaker) group in check. Such is the case in South Africa today, and in Ireland.

For more than seven hundred years the Catholics in Northern Ireland have waged bloody battles against their British colonizers. The Statutes of Kilkenny, enacted in 1366 and not repealed until 1829, forbade marriage between the English and the Irish; nor might any English subject speak Gaelic, the language of the Irish. Under the Protestant King William III, Prince of Orange, a set of laws known as the Penal Code was enacted to oppress and degrade the Irish people. (The Penal Code was the model used by the U.S. Southern states in drafting segregation laws.) Catholics were forbidden to vote or to hold office. They were prohibited from entering military or civil service, the legal profession, or teaching. Catholic schools were banned. A Catholic could not own a horse worth more than five pounds; if he did have such a horse, a Protestant could take it away from him. The right of religious practice was severely restricted; mass was celebrated secretly in private homes and in the fields while men stood guard to watch for British patrols.

One of the laws in the Penal Code prohibited a Catholic from willing his entire farm to one son. The farm had to be divided among all the sons. This resulted in the division of small farms into tracts of land too small to support a family. A great number of Protestant landowners, newly rich and greedy, amassed huge estates on which they built magnificent castles and country mansions. Meanwhile the large Catholic majority lived at the starvation level.

A disease of potato plants called blight destroyed three years of crops. Thus, in 1841, a severe famine killed one million Irish Catholics whose staple food was the potato. The beef, pork, wheat, and oats produced in Ireland were reserved for export. The starving Irish families were not aided by the British. Thus between the years 1846 and 1851 more than a million Irish Catholics emigrated to the United States.

Sadly, the Irish in their new land of freedom became the oppressors of black Americans. In the early 1900s a black man walking through an Irish neighborhood on St. Patrick's Day (in New York City) would be set upon and beaten by Irish toughs. Even the Roman Catholic Church, which was then controlled by the Irish in the United States, discriminated against blacks. In recent years the Church has moved to rectify those discriminatory practices. During the 1960s Roman Catholics took a strong stand for the enactment of civil rights laws.

It is interesting that in New York City, Protestant religious schools were supported with public taxes. The practice was ended in 1878 when Catholics began demanding their share of the educational "pie" for the growing number of Catholic schools being established for the children of Irish immigrants.

The Black American

Slavery of African blacks began in the New World in 1607 and continued for 258 years. Slavery ended after the Civil War with the Emancipation Proclamation in 1863 and the ratification of the Thirteenth Amendment in 1865. Based on the fourteenth-century Penal Code that was used against the Catholics in Ireland, the governments of the thirteen Southern states created what were called Black Codes. Although varying slightly in each state, the Black Codes deprived the newly freed blacks of the right to vote, hold office, serve on juries, testify in court against whites, or assemble without official permission.

Of paramount importance in the Codes of all former Confederate states were regulations restricting the freedom of blacks to work. In South Carolina black men were required to purchase a special license at a cost of ten to one hundred dollars per year for any job except farm laborer or servant. The Code in Mississippi prohibited the renting or leasing of land by blacks. The Louisiana Code mandated that all farm workers make contracts with farm owners (employers) during the first ten days of each January; not until the expiration of the contract could workers leave their employers. The Black Codes were responsible for economic deprivation of black people, who worked for little or no pay while the white plantation owners became wealthy. When a person is unable to earn a living, he is economically weakened. This, in turn, weakens him psychologically, and he is not able to struggle for political or social rights.

Job discrimination and exclusion from even menial work has been the dreadful legacy of each generation of American black males since Reconstruction days. The pattern of job denial to black males has been woven into the economic fabric of this country so tightly and so consistently that there has been no workplace for them. Whereas immigrants from southern and eastern Europe were feared because of their threat as competitors in the job market, the American black male was systematically denied the opportunity to compete. When the slaves were freed from agricultural work where they had served as beasts of burden, few had skills that were useful in other areas of work. After slavery, every opportunity to become skilled was denied. Today there exists in the United States an underclass of black males who are unemployed and unemployable because they lack skills and education. Excerpts from an article that appeared in the New York *Times* give statistical evidence of the tragic effects of chronic unemployment:

OUTLOOK FOR YOUNG BLACK MALES CALLED BLEAK

Speakers and panelists at the NAACP Legal Defense and Education Fund's annual Civil Rights Institute painted a gloomy picture of economic and educational progress for most blacks in recent years.... In a panel discussion titled "Young Black Males: An Endangered Species," the statistics that appear below were cited:

50% of young blacks are unemployed; 25% under the age of 25 have *never held a job*; 1 in 6 has been arrested by the age of 19; more than 10,000 black males between the ages of 15 and 19 die each year in homicides; up to 72% of black males in New York City drop out of high school; among the blacks between the ages of 20 and 24 there are only 45 marriageable males for every 100 females, largely because of unemployment and incarceration.

Chapter 5 contains a more detailed discussion of the impoverished black family, including reasons for the chronic unemployment of the masses of black males. Currently, public and private agencies are bringing into focus the plight of the impoverished black family. Breaking the cycle of unemployment that has plagued them for generations requires massive effort by the government and the private sector.

The South African Black

In 1948, just after World War II, the Nationalist government in South Africa announced a policy of *apartheid*, the complete separation of the races. The segregation established under apartheid was far more rigorous than that of the existing laws. The policy of *baasskap*, bosshood, had been traditional in the old Dutch settlements in South Africa.

Apartheid is a comprehensive system of separating the black African from the white population in every imaginable aspect of life. As expressed by Daniel F. Malan, South Africa's prime minister from 1948 to 1954: ". . . Theoretically, the object of the policy of apartheid could be achieved by dividing the country into two parts with all the whites in one and all the blacks in the other. For the foreseeable future, this is simply not practical politics . . . ."

The laws of apartheid are numerous and overlapping to close any loopholes that might have escaped notice. As new separatist laws are needed, they are drawn up and enacted. The Separate Representation of Voters Bill prevents direct participation in the political process by either the black or the "colored" population. Numerous measures enforce segregation in parks, railroad stations, buses, post offices, beaches, public buildings, theaters, movie houses, and restaurants.

To promote "racial purity," the Prohibition of Mixed Marriages Act was passed to prevent intermarriage between white and black persons. In the same vein, the Immorality Act imposes severe penalties for sexual intercourse between whites and nonwhites. The Population Registration Act, passed in 1950, ordered not only the racial classification of the entire population, but also the issuing of identity cards that state whether one is white, black, or colored.

In 1956 the Industrial Conciliation Act put into effect an interlacing network of restrictions that prohibit black Africans from doing any work that is considered skilled. Thus, black men are confined to jobs that are semiskilled or unskilled: A black may drive a lightweight truck, but heavy trucking is reserved for whites.

Freedom of movement by the black African is limited by a series of "pass" laws that require a permit to go into certain areas. If a black man is permitted to live in an area near his work, his wife may not join him and keep house for him. Consequently, the black rural villages are peopled by women and children in households from which the husbands and fathers have been removed by the hated pass laws. The Group Areas Act and the Natives Urban Areas Act prohibit urban land ownership by black South Africans. Specifically, the Group Areas Act designates and controls the segregated areas in which all nonwhites must live. When this law was passed, numerous nonwhites were uprooted because the sections in which they lived were reassigned to whites.

The life of the black majority in South Africa is harsh, bitter, and difficult. Apartheid is an all-encompassing system that controls every aspect of life. The work that is open to black Africans is limited, and for long hours of hard work they are paid a fraction of what a white person would receive. The conditions of life for blacks in South Africa are best likened to semislavery. Once employed, a man cannot quit his job to take a new one. He cannot form or join a labor union, and he does not receive medical benefits or a pension. Education is separate and of poor quality. The schools are overcrowded, understaffed, and underfunded. Books are scarce. Education for black children is limited to their function as future unskilled workers.

Jews

Jews have a long history of persecution. They are a dispersed people, having had to flee from their persecutors since ancient times. The scope of this book does not permit discussion of ancient Jewish history, but this section will examine the effects of hostility toward the Jews beginning with the Middle Ages.

During the Middle Ages (A.D. 500–1500), Jews in many European countries were increasingly subjected to repressive and restrictive laws. Jews were not allowed to own land and were restricted to enclosed sections of towns called ghettos. They were not permitted to join the artisans' guilds and had to pay dearly for protection from some rulers. The Church forbade any contact between Jews and Christians. It was during the reign of Pope Innocent III in 1215 that Jews were ordered to wear the yellow Jews' Badge. During the Crusades entire Jewish communities in Germany and France were exterminated. In 1290 the Jews were expelled from England after having been stripped of their belongings.

During the Golden Age (A.D. 950–1250) Jews together with Moslems developed an enlightened civilization when the Moors ruled Spain. Things changed, however, in 1492. Under the reign of Queen Isabella and King Ferdinand, an Edict of Expulsion was issued that required Jews to convert to Christianity or leave the country. About two hundred thousand Jews left Spain, migrating to Italy, Holland, and the New World.

The year 1815 ushered in a wave of German-Jewish

The stoning of Jews in Spain circa 1492 (The New York Public Library Picture Collection).

migration that was to last until 1877. Jews in Germany, Austria, and Hungary were subject to a great number of discriminatory practices. Besides being forced to live in ghettos and denied the right to own land, Jews were required to pay a special tax known as a "Jew toll" whenever they left the ghetto. The right of marriage was granted only to the eldest sibling to keep down the growth of the Jewish population. A large number of Central European Jews migrated to the United States.

The Eastern European Jewish migration took place between 1880 and 1925. Once again Jews suffered persecution in Russia, Poland, Lithuania, and Austria-Hungary. The most serious of the discriminatory practices were the pogroms, government-initiated massacres of Jews that took place in cities such as Kiev, Odessa, and Warsaw. Under Czar Nicholas II of Russia, numerous Jews were killed in a pogrom that lasted for three days. Jews from the Eastern European countries migrated to the United States. Currently, some two million Jews in Russia are targets of systematic discrimination.

The persecution of Jews continued in the twentieth century. In Nazi Germany, under the dictatorship of Adolf Hitler, Jews were deprived of rights and life. They were deprived of German citizenship and forbidden to intermarry with Christians. Jews were not allowed to write or publish, act on the stage or in movies, teach, work in banks, give concerts, work in hospitals, or enter labor or professional organizations. They were barred from participating in civic activities and were ineligible for unemployment insurance. It was commonly accepted that towns had the right to prevent Jews from living within their boundaries.

The persecution of Jews in Nazi Germany escalated into government-directed violence against every known Jew living within the borders of Germany or in German-occupied countries. Organized mobs looted Jewish shops, burned synagogues, invaded Jewish homes, and beat Jews on the streets. Jews were forced to wear a yellow Star of David. Beginning in 1942, the Nazis began a systematic annihilation of Jews. Less than 20 percent of the 600,000 Jews of Germany were able to escape. Germany murdered over 6 million European Jews. As an example of man's inhumanity to man, few non-Jewish Germans protested the massive persecution. Many non-German Europeans actively cooperated with the Germans in their plan to exterminate European Jewry. However, there were organized underground groups that helped thousands of Jews escape from Germany and German-occupied countries.

The close of World II saw mass migrations of Jews to the United States and Israel.

Chinese

The discovery of gold in California in 1849 had as a direct result the importation of cheap labor from China. By 1852 some 25,000 Chinese were living on the West Coast. They continued to migrate to the United States from China at the rate of 4,000 per year. At the end of the 1870s some 150,000 Chinese were living in California alone. The Taiping rebellion of 1850 and the constant demand for laborers to work in building the Central Pacific Railway further stimulated Chinese immigration to the United States.

American workers became increasingly resentful of the Chinese laborers, viewing them as a menace to their jobs. Men from China accepted low pay, had the stamina to work long hours, and in general were not difficult to manage.

An Irish-born agitator, Dennis Kearney, initiated an anti-Chinese movement in California. Of course, the basis of the movement was racial prejudice. The white population resented the Chinese because they clung to their religion and way of life. Their exotic dress, customs, and language and their intention of returning to China with money earned in the U.S. fanned the flames of hostility against them. The California Workingmen's Party spearheaded the demand for legislation to prohibit further Chinese immigration.

In 1882 Congress passed the Chinese Exclusion Act, which prohibited Chinese laborers from entering the United States for a period of ten years. The act was extended in 1902 and made permanent in 1904. The Chinese population in the United States declined from 107,000 in 1890 to 75,000 in 1930.

Japanese

Japanese immigration was not viewed as a serious problem until the early 1900s. At the turn of the century, there were fewer than 25,000 Japanese in the United States. Around 1904, however, an upturn in Japanese immigration alarmed people living on the Pacific coast. Their reaction was to pass restrictive laws that prevented Japanese from owning property or leasing real estate.

In 1907 President Theodore Roosevelt reached a "gentlemen's agreement" with the Japanese government to discourage immigration of its laboring classes to the United States. In exchange, the San Francisco school board withdrew an order barring Japanese children from attending school. However, a small but steady stream of Japanese immigrants continued to trickle into California. The Immigration Act of 1924 put an end to Japanese immigration.

Habits of suspicion and distrust die hard, however. In 1941, after the Japanese bombing of Pearl Harbor had catapulted the United States into World War II, some 112,000 persons of Japanese ancestry—although born and bred Americans—were removed from their homes and possessions and herded into internment camps for the duration of the war.

Restrictive Immigration Acts

Beginning in the 1920s and continuing to 1952, a series of laws were enacted to limit immigration to persons from favored countries. Underlying these restrictive acts was the prejudicial theme of Nordic supremacy, a theory holding that immigrants from Northern and Western Europe were superior to those from Eastern and Southern Europe. Many of those empowered to make these laws were disappointed by the failure of Poles, Russians, Italians, and Jews to "Americanize" rapidly enough to create the mythical "melting pot" instead of the more realistic "mixing bowl." There was also fear among the working class that unrestricted immigration would jeopardize the jobs of Americans.

A summary of the restrictive immigration laws follows:

1921 Emergency Quota Act	Limited immigration in any one year to 3 percent of the number of foreign-born residents of that nationality living in the U.S. in 1910.
1924 Johnson-Reed Act	Reduced the national quotas to 2 percent and excluded all Asians.
1929 National Origins Clause	Limited total immigrants to 150,000 and assigned each country a quota of that total. The minimum quota per country was 100. Asians were excluded.
1952 Immigration and Nationality Act	Continued the national origins quota but increased the total immigration to 156,000. A token quota of 2,000 was assigned to the Far East and Pacific areas. Members of Communist countries were barred.

The 1965 amendments to the Immigration Act corrected the racist thinking of the earlier acts. Currently many more people are being admitted from areas that formerly had low quotas, such as the West Indies, African and Arab countries, Greece, Portugal, the Philippine Republic, and Italy.

Native Americans

The opening of the far West for settlement by the white population was accomplished by systematic and vicious destruction of the Indian tribes that had lived for generations in the region that now constitutes the Western states. Inhabiting the Northwest were the Sioux, Blackfoot, Crow, Cheyenne, and Arapaho. Occupying the Southwest territories were the Comanche, Kiowa, Ute, Southern Cheyenne, Apache, and Southern Arapaho. For generations these strong and warlike tribes had built their lives around the millions of buffalo that roamed the open range, providing food, hides, lariats, bowstrings, and fuel.

The gold rush of 1849 ushered in the first wave of white migration. In 1850 there were 100,000 California Indians; ten years later their number had been reduced to 35,000. The fate of the California Indians foretold what was to happen to all of the other Indian tribes that inhabited the West. Historians cite the three catastrophic events that led to the destruction of the once proud Indian empires. Most serious of those events was the destruction of the buffalo herds, without which the life-style that had evolved over generations of time was ruptured. turning the Indians into rootless, starving vagabonds. Second was the perfection of the Colt repeating revolver, which increased the efficiency of warfare in the Plains. Third, many Indians died as a result of the spread of smallpox and venereal diseases.

Beginning in 1861, massive invasions of the Indian hunting grounds by miners and white homesteaders began the numerous conflicts that were to destroy Indian tribes. In 1862 the Sioux Indians who lived in the Dakota region went on the warpath, massacring or imprisoning thousands of white men, women, and children. In 1864, in retaliation for the Indians' attack on a stagecoach, a Colonel Chivington directed a savage slaughter of Cheyenne Indian men, women, and children that horrified the entire nation.

And so the advance progressed: Indian attack followed by white slaughter. The Indian attacks were designed to preserve the hunting grounds. Tribe after tribe was decimated. The attempt of the Sioux to preserve their hunting grounds led to the 1876 massacre of General George Custer's regiment on the banks of the Little Big Horn. The retaliation against the Sioux was relentless.

The temperament of the tribe had little to do with the degree of its survival. The mild-mannered, peace-loving Nez Percé tribe of western Idaho suffered at the hands of marauding hordes of white men, who swarmed over their hunting grounds in search of gold. Those of the tribe not killed were driven from their homeland and forced to live in the unfamiliar lands of the Southwest. At the time of the final defeat, Chief Joseph uttered these words for his tribe:

I am tired of fighting. Our chiefs are killed . . . He who led the young men is dead. It is cold and we have no blankets. The little children are freezing to death. My people, some of them, have run away to the hills and have no blankets, no food . . . . Hear me, my chiefs. My heart is sick and sad. I am tired . . . ."

Few full-blooded Indians remain. About 450,000 of those who claim Indian ancestry live on reservations, mainly in the Western states. It is believed that between 200,000 and 500,000 Indians live in the cities. Judging by the quality of life on the reservations, the American Indian is the most oppressed and the poorest of the minorities in the United States. The school dropout rate is twice as great as the national average. Unemployment of the males is nearly twelve times as great as that of whites.

In recent years, reservation Indians have begun to respond to the civil rights movement and to make demands for improvement. The more educated and more militant Indians on the reservations are seeking improvements in the schools and struggling for the right to control their own affairs in respect to land ownership and federal programs. The term "Indian Power" is being used by the younger, more forceful generations who are striving to improve conditions on the reservations and to obtain for the Indian people what is rightfully theirs.

Coping with Discrimination

How does one cope with discrimination that is sanctioned by law? A person on his own cannot challenge discriminatory codes, but many people together can raise the public consciousness about racial justice. Harold Fleming is a white Southerner who has spent forty years fighting for the civil rights of black people. As executive director of the Southern Regional Council and president of the Potomac Institute, he worked with organizations that sought to eliminate discrimination and move away from segregation. He also served in the Johnson administration as deputy director of the United States Community Relations Service and was chairman of the National Committee against Discrimination in Housing. Fleming was able to work with and influence people who were shapers of public opinion, who could make a segment of society recognize the harm that prejudice does. Through his efforts and those of a great many people throughout the United States, and by nonviolent means, discriminatory laws of segregation were declared illegal.

Apartheid in South Africa is regarded as an abomination. As violence escalates in the cities of Johannesburg, Pretoria, and Durban, enlightened nations are talking about divestment, the removal of investments from South Africa. The tightly interwoven network of discriminatory laws and the jailing and silencing of black leaders mean that the black people of South Africa cannot get freedom without violence. The violence has begun: White killing black, black killing white, and black killing black. The black and "colored" population have also had violent clashes. However, some saner voices have begun to be heard. Bishop Desmond Tutu was awarded the Nobel Prize for Peace for his nonviolent efforts to resist apartheid. White South African businessmen have called for an end to the system. People worldwide are championing the cause of a free South Africa.

World wide protests, including economic sanctions of South Africa, have led to the easing of some of the discriminatory restrictions. Nelson Mandela, the anti-apartheid leader who was jailed in 1962 was released from prison in February, 1990.

CHAPTER 2

The Results of Prejudice

When one group of human beings feels superior to another group because of differences in race, religion, sex, social status, or ethnic origin, a group attitude or mind-set shapes the thinking of the "superior" group. Depending upon the intensity of feeling, a set of behaviors is adopted that express the attitude of being "better than." Political and economic strength determine the extent and the form that the acting-out will take.

The process of prejudice is usually motivated by hostility and deep-seated resentment that develops strong roots in a culture. A most telling current example is the deep-seated hatred of the Afrikaners for the South African blacks. The original hostility was generated by fear that the blacks by sheer numbers would overpower the white population. Harsh repressive measures weakened and divided them so that a white minority population cruelly controls the black majority. The original attitude of fear

Exploitation of immigrants is a serious outcome of prejudice. Italian immigrants (circa 1872) being sold overpriced food.

has been translated over time into violent hatred of blacks. Hatred is an emotion that denies one's exercise of balanced reason.

Prejudice seems to be a generic failing of humankind. In one form or another it has been used throughout history to control the progress of minority groups. In the United States, blacks, Jews, Mexicans, Irish Catholics, Italians, Puerto Ricans, Asians, and a host of other immigrant groups have been subjected to the unfair practices brought on by prejudice.

At the turn of the century, immigrants from Southern and Eastern Europe were considered unwanted minorities. They experienced difficulty in finding work, in obtaining housing, and even in gaining the full protection of the law. The established Americans considered the

European immigrants inferior and resented their strange customs and folkways. Many working-class Americans feared that the immigrants would work for lower wages and thus take away their jobs. Therefore, the newcomers were subjected to acts of prejudice and discrimination.

To exert control, the dominant group uses a series of "reasonable" devices against the weaker group that give psychological support to unreasonable acts. The first such device is the use of the law to deny the target group due legal process. Laws are passed to prohibit the earning of a living and basic civil rights. Chapter 1 cited examples of how the means of earning a living were denied to Jews in Europe, to black Americans, and to the blacks in South Africa. Another such device is the use of religion to support acts of hostility. The Inquisition in fifteenth-century Spain exterminated Jews who refused to convert to Christianity. Before passage of the Civil Rights Act of 1964, the Christian denominations in the American South supported segregation. Religious groups use Scripture to justify their posture of prejudice and the resulting acts of violence and repression. In common practice, the psychological weapons of *stereotyping* and *scapegoating* are used against groups to reinforce negative mind-sets.

Stereotyping

A stereotype is a mental picture that one group has of another, a false characterization designed to degrade the target group. Early in life stereotypes become fixed in a person's mind and are reinforced by similar caricatures in the mass media. A painful case in point: American movies made from the 1920s to the 1940s depicted the black American male in the Stepin Fetchit image, a man-boy buffoon afraid of the dark and of low intelligence. During the same period the Mexicans fared no better. They were characterized either as lazy creatures always sleeping under their sombreros, or as vicious killers who wore a bandolier of bullets draped across their chests. American Indians suffered their share of negative stereo-typing: killers on the rampage, burning and pillaging the settlements of the noble white homesteaders. Throughout the four decades of movie-making, Italian-American males have been portrayed as gangsters; sometimes they sang opera and ate enormous plates of spaghetti, but always they were involved in crime and killing.

Until the mid-1950s, when the National Association for the Advancement of Colored People (NAACP) raised public consciousness, a great many household articles bore racist caricatures of blacks, depicting them as lazy, unreliable, or prone to crime. "Rastus," a familiar turn-of-the-century caricature, appeared in hundreds of adver-tisements for Cream of Wheat cereal. Always in chef's whites, smiling and servile, Rastus dished out steaming bowls of cereal to the white folks.

Black women were often portrayed as "mammies," their features excessively broadened. The mammy was a trade-mark for Aunt Jemima's Pancake Flour for many years until the image was modernized. Often the black stereotypes had themes of violence toward children. A famous bisque piece shows a black male child climbing a tree while a dog nips at his bottom. Another example of violence toward black children were the ashtrays, circa 1930, that placed children near the yawning jaws of alligators. A popular myth was that alligators had a particular taste for black flesh. A pervasive caricature ever present until the late 1950s was the black male (man or boy) biting into watermelon. So painful was this stereotype that many middle-aged and older blacks today will not eat watermelon!

Stereotyping hurts individuals and groups. A false picture serves as evidence of the unworthiness of a group or of an individual who belongs to a stereotyped group. On the basis of negative characterizations, society typecasts people into roles that they, indeed, may not play. During the busing controversy that took place in many American cities during the late 1970s, Italian-Americans were often depicted as bigots threatening busloads of black children who were brought to their neighborhoods. In truth, Italian-Americans tend to remain in changing areas. In New York City, they comprise the largest white population that has remained in the city, not migrating to the suburbs.

Of recent years, black males have been stereotyped as muggers, pimps, dope pushers, and for-hire killers. In truth, the number of blacks who commit such crimes represent an infinitesimal portion of the total black male population. Most blacks are law-abiding people who also suffer at the hands of an unruly few.

Stereotyping leads to inappropriate value judgments about the worth and progress of an entire race. A self-published book written by a retired physicist contains this statement: " . . . as long as American blacks insist on preserving their jungle freedoms, their women, their avoidance of personal responsibility and their abhorrence of the work ethic, there will be a continuing minority problem and a continuing erosion of our society." The author fails to mention how discriminatory practices in the workplace have contributed to this "unwillingness to work" trait so commonly attributed to black males. It is not uncommon for black males to suffer severe harassment from white workers. The following news item is a case in point:

For almost nine years, Ben Citchen says, he went to work dreading what the day might bring: a dead rat in his lunchpail, a noose hung over his work station. His car was vandalized and racial slurs were scribbled on the floor and walls near where he worked.

. . . the eight-member Michigan Civil Rights Commission decided he had been racially harassed on his job . . . in violation of Michigan's civil rights. They ordered the company to pay him $1.5 million in damages.

The physicist-author quoted above fails to mention that economic cutbacks by Republican administrations have hurt black males. The closing down of major American manufacturing plants, including steel mills and automobile assembly plants, and the movement of manufacturing industries to countries outside of the United States have left a large segment of the population unemployed. As the last to be hired, blacks are the first to be fired, and that has made them vulnerable to conditions of job erosion.

Scapegoating

Assigning blame to a powerless minority group for things that have gone wrong in government or for other misfortunes that have touched a community is called *scapegoating*. In 1348, when the bubonic plague swept through Europe, Jews were accused of poisoning the drinking water and thus were held responsible for the devastating epidemic. Within recent history, notorious examples of scapegoating were prepetrated by the Nazis, who blamed the Jews for all of Germany's economic troubles following World War I. The Nazis used the scapegoating propaganda to support the violent acts of persecution that led to the extermination of six million Jews.

At the outbreak of World War II, the United States made a serious mistake based on the erroneous belief that Japanese-Americans living on the West Coast would be disloyal to this country. The belief, based on prejudice and scapegoating, caused the government to intern Japanese-Americans in relocation camps. With less than a week's notice many Japanese-American families had to dispose of their property and personal effects and move to inland camps. In truth, the vast majority of the Japanese-American population were loyal, and many of the men made splendid contributions in the armed forces.

Historically, the black American has been subjected to the pressures of discrimination and prejudice for all of the years following the signing of the Emancipation Proclamation in 1863. The myths of scapegoating have harmed black people in the past and continue to do so. One such myth is that when white employment decreases, the employment of blacks increases, implying that black workers take jobs away from whites. Another such myth is that black young people are given preference in college admissions. The statistics that follow dispel many other black/white myths.

Facts on Black/White Disparities

- In 1969, 29 percent of the nation's poor population was black; in 1981, the percentage was 27.5.
- In 1980, 11.4 percent of whites under seventeen years of age lived in poverty, while 41.6 percent of blacks under seventeen lived in poverty.
- Of total welfare payments made in 1988, blacks received 36 percent. About 77 percent of all black families received no public assistance.
- In 1950 there were 29.9 deaths per thousand among

white infants under one year old and 53.7 deaths per thousand among black infants under one year old. By 1980 infant mortality among whites had fallen by 59.9 percent to 12 per thousand, while that of blacks had fallen by 54.4 percent to 24.5 per thousand.

- In 1988, 47 percent of white families were middle class, while 24 percent of black families were middle class. In 1979, 50 percent of white families were middle class compared to 24 percent of black families.
- In 1969, black firms received 0.22% percent of total business receipts in the U.S. By 1977 the figure had declined to 0.19 percent.
- In 1976 blacks represented 6 percent of graduate school students and 4.5 percent of professional school students.
- In 1968–69 blacks represented 2.2 percent of college faculty; in 1977, 4.4 percent.

Psychological Effects of Discrimination

Prejudice brings with it discrimination, acts that deny others fair treatment. Discrimination has strong psychological effects on people in the target group, whose daily lives are circumscribed by restrictive laws and practices. Psychologists tell us that one of the results of discrimination is an *oppression psychosis*. A person feeling the weight of prejudice regards himself and other members of his race or ethnic group as inferior to the majority group. The acceptance of the status of inferior person has many detrimental effects on his behavior. For many black children, especially boys, feelings of inferiority affect their ability to learn. The "reading block" syndrome is quite

common in ghetto children, who experience great difficulty with the language arts. Oppression psychosis causes
many people to see prejudice and discrimination where
none exists. It becomes difficult for them to accept the
friendship of others of another racial, ethnic, or religious
group, expecting hurt and exploitation. Children whose
parents were imprisoned in concentration camps are
familiar with their parents' depression and episodes of
withdrawal from the family. That same behavior is characteristic of black women, single heads of households
laboring under oppression psychosis, who withdraw to
relieve the pain of prejudice.

In direct opposition to withdrawal is the overly aggressive behavior that becomes a way of life for many oppressed peoples. The hostile and vicious gangs that form
in ghetto areas are evidence of a psychotic aggressiveness.
Among many oppressed people, family violence becomes
a way of life. This is true among South African blacks and
among the American blacks, Hispanics, and Irish who
comprise the poorer end of the population. Seemingly
without hope and depressed by the force of discrimination,
many people become hostile, ready for a fight, and unable
to react calmly and rationally to minor changes in their
daily lives. They live at the edge of anger and are triggered
into explosive action by an event that they regard as an act
of prejudice. Recently in Birmingham, England, the police
raided the house of a woman believed to be carrying on
some illegal activity. In the course of the raid, the woman
died of a heart attack. This led to nine days of rioting,
burning, rock-throwing, and even killing between the
black West Indian population and the whites who lived in
that district. The riots in Birmingham were reminiscent of
those that took place during the 1960s and 1970s in the
Watts section of Los Angeles, Washington, D.C., and

Newark, New Jersey, where rioters regarded themselves as forcefully demanding their civil rights.

The results of prejudice are terrible. As Chapter 3 reveals, the formation of hate groups is a serious consequence of prejudice.

CHAPTER ◇ 3

Hate Systems

Organized vs. Unorganized Hate Systems

A devastating result of prejudice is the spawning of hate systems. A hate system is a functioning, cohesive group organized for the purpose of carrying out acts of violence against persons who do not meet their racial, religious, or ethnic criteria. Such groups want to be seen and heard and identified with their ideology. Most of them adopt a paramilitary structure, wear uniforms, strut around with guns, and spew forth racial venom in printed tracts or verbally at rallies. The existence of such groups is common knowledge, a circumstance that offers protection to those against whom they "wage war": People can protect themselves from known hazards.

More insidious is the unorganized hate system. Although the unorganized hate system is not constituted in a formal group, a *group mind* directs the thinking almost as if the group were organized. Sometimes people who are closely connected to one another through a work situation adopt the group mind and act as a group in violence. An account of harassment of a black man by white workers was given in Chapter 1. As another example, a group of building construction workers are at different places on a job site, yet they act spontaneously to attack a group of young people who are demonstrating against a social injustice. The job product of these workers is unrelated to social issues, yet the group mind or psyche arouses in each worker an immediate hostile response.

Sometimes the group mind controls even when people are not physically in contact, but are unified by a common goal. Unethical real estate dealers in a given area may decide to "blockbust" by urging whites to sell their homes because blacks or some other ethnic group are moving in. If words don't work, these dealers often resort to other tactics. Real estate developers wanting tenants to vacate large apartment houses often hire thugs, drug addicts, prostitutes, and other criminal types to make conditions in the buildings so unbearable that the tenants will move.

Of recent concern has been the working of the hate system in police departments, which inevitably leads to police brutality. Examples are seen in the brutal beating of a black motorist by L.A. police video taped by a bystander or the young California athlete who, having been stopped for a minor traffic violation, was choked to death by an illegal stranglehold used by the arresting policemen. These acts constitute a hidden kind of terrorism against which one has no protection. In Dallas, Texas, engineer Lenell Geter was given a life sentence for armed robbery when, in fact, he was working at his job in sight of many witnesses when the robbery took place. Racism and sloppy police work were to blame for his false arrest and conviction. Although Geter's conviction was overturned and he was released from prison, he suffered needlessly through months of trial and wrongful incarceration.

In each of the cases cited above, there was not *one* act of violence perpetrated by one policeman against one victim, but an entire system was called into play to defend the officer. In one case, the evidence of workers at the electronic firm supporting the whereabouts of the engineer was not allowed at his trial. The family of the athlete pressed for evidence through a far-too-intricate system of court orders and hearings to prove that the youth was killed brutally and needlessly. The hidden hate systems are difficult to anticipate. A black man cannot walk through life in constant fear that he might be stopped for a minor infraction of the law and be killed before he reaches the precinct. Therefore built into our police and judicial systems must be unshakable safeguards that will limit and discourage the opportunities for police violence against a detainee.

Organized Hate Groups

Most of the organized hate groups in the United States have at their core the concept of *white supremacy*. According to this belief system, the white race is inherently superior to all others and therefore should have control of all economic and political power. The emotion of hate is hard to control. It spreads out and touches many facets of society. Therefore white-supremacy hate groups hate not only blacks but also Jews, Catholics, "liberals," and anyone who is working for social change. (In recent years, the hatred against Catholics seems to be diminishing.)

The concept of white supremacy probably started in the United States around 1660 when the slave codes were enacted by colonial legislatures controlled by wealthy men. Forty years later great numbers of Africans were being kidnapped and brought as slaves to the southern colonies.

From then until the signing of the Thirteenth Amendment in 1865, slavery was an integral part of the political, economic, and social fabric of society in the United States. Following the Civil War and the freeing of the slaves, a secret organization called the Ku Klux Klan was formed. Its purpose was to restore white supremacy in the South through acts of terrorism against blacks and those whites who were working toward the establishment of democracy.

Ku Klux Klan

Headed by a former slave trader, Nathan Bedford Forrest, the Ku Klux Klan in 1867 became a night-riding vigilante group, enlarging its numbers by appealing to poor whites through prejudice and white supremacy. The uniform of hooded white or black robes and masks hid the identity of the Klansmen while they committed atrocities. They beat their victims—men, women, children, blacks and whites who supported the efforts of blacks toward democracy— and filled the bleeding wounds with hot tar. They killed their victims by lynching: hanging the person from a tree and setting him afire. They burned down houses, destroyed black churches, raped women, and committed acts of brutality against men.

The Ku Klux Klan has remained in existence for nearly 125 years, experiencing periods of decline followed by spurts of revival. When things in the United States are going well—high employment, little social change, political status quo—the Klan becomes quiescent. During times of social change, however, Klan membership increases markedly. A review of Klan history reveals that the periods following the Civil War, World War I, and World War II and the periods of the civil rights movement of the 1960s, women's rights in the 1970s, and the gay rights

Violence is a dastardly outcome of prejudice. Torturing and lynching of black Americans was a common occurrence in the Southern States prior to the passage of the Civil Rights Act of 1964. The lynching shown here took place in 1938. (Schomburg Center for Research in Black Culture, The New York Public Library, Astor, Lenox and Tilden Foundations)

movement of the 1980s stimulated Klan membership significantly.

At the core of the social issues that motivate Klan activity is the challenge to white supremacy from blacks and other nonwhites. In recent years the struggle for civil liberties has grown to encompass other minority groups: Asians, native Americans, Puerto Ricans, Chicanos, women, gay men, lesbian women, disabled people, and senior citizens. The pursuit of civil rights and political freedom by diverse groups that make up society in the United States is most unsettling to some people. In the South and in other areas of the country, politicians, clergy, legislators, doctors, lawyers, and merchants do not want a shift in the balance of power in their communities. Many of the "pillars of society" have given strong financial support to the Klan. The Klan "soldiers" are mostly poor white men and some women who, enticed by the rhetoric of racial prejudice, do the bidding of the groups in power, who remain in respectability behind the scenes. That behind-the-scenes goading of Klansmen by influential members of a community is described by a former Klan member:

> . . . One day I was walkin' downtown and a certain city council member saw me comin'. I expected him to shake my hand because he was talkin' to me at night on the telephone. I had been in his home and visited with him. He crossed the street to avoid me . . . . I began to think, somethin's wrong here. Most of 'em are merchants or maybe an attorney, an insurance agent, people like that. As long as they kept the low-income whites and the low-income blacks fightin', they're gonna maintain control. I began to get that feelin' after I was ignored in public. I thought . . . you're not gonna use me anymore."

The Anti-Defamation League of B'nai B'rith provides some startling figures about Klan membership in the 1990s: about 10,000 with 100,000 sympathizers. The Ku Klux Klan is made up of several factions that compete with each other for membership and power. According to figures estimated in 1980, the largest factions are as follows:

The United Klans of America	3,500–4,000 members
The Invisible Empire, Knights of the KKK	2,000–2,500 members
The Knights of the KKK	1,500–2,000 members
The Confederation of the Independent Order of the Knights of the KKK	1,500 members

The Ku Klux Klan is spread throughout the United States and carries on active recruitment activities in twenty-two states. The theme of the Klan's recruitment and the core of its purpose is to promote white supremacy through acts of terrorism. Its literature calls for death of Jews, persons of color, gay people, and whites who are working toward democracy. The Klan is no longer as anti-Catholic as it once was, and some factions even invite Catholic membership, However, the Klan is violently opposed to the efforts of women to win equal rights and also opposes equal rights for immigrants.

The Klan stirs up racial tensions and religious hatreds, as shown by the news items that follow: During the 1980s vandalism increased against Jewish places of worship and anti-Semitic violence promoted by the Klan. A Klan youth group attacked patrons in a gay bar in Oklahoma City. The flames of hatred were fanned by the KKK in the process of desegregation of the Boston public schools in 1980. The outrage still smolders in the offices of the Greensboro

Members of the Invisible Empire, Knights of the KKK, crossing the Edmund Pettus Bridge at Selma, Alabama. The bridge is where black demonstrators were beaten by Alabama state troopers in 1965 as they tried to march to Montgomery in support of their right to vote. (Bill Stanton, Klanwatch Project).

(North Carolina) Justice Fund against six Klansmen and three members of the American Nazi Party, who massacred five Communists, four white men, and one black woman. These members of the Communist Workers Party were shot down in cold blood at a political rally. After an all-white jury acquitted the defendants of murder, there was a sharp increase in Klan membership in North Carolina. Said one observer, "The acquittals are dangerous to all Americans. The message is that it's okay to kill people if you don't like their political views."

Protest against the Ku Klux Klan by a predominantly black crowd in Decatur, Alabama (Bill Stanton, Klanwatch Project).

A Who's Who of Other Hate Groups

In addition to the Ku Klux Klan, currently operating in the United States are nine other white-supremacy hate groups linked to and rivaled by each other. A brief description of each group follows:

The *Aryan Nations* was founded in the 1940s and established in northern Idaho in 1973. It operates a national white supremacist computer bulletin board that gives "how to" instructions for getting racist messages on cable TV. Messages of hate include claims that illegal aliens are plotting to overthrow the United States. The computer network is designed to circumvent Canadian law that prohibits the distribution of hate literature. The hub of this group's activities is training its members to commit violent acts. Many of its members have been convicted of carrying illegal weapons.

The *Euro-American Alliance* was founded in the 1980s and is headquartered in Milwaukee. This group has announced its intention to defend Aryan Nations members against counterattacks by the Jewish Defense Organization.

The *Order*, also known as *the White American Bastion* and *Bruder Schweigen*, German for "Silent Brotherhood," was founded in the early 1980s and is primarily active in the Northwest. It is an offshoot of the Aryan Nations and is believed responsible for the killing of a Jewish radio talkshow host in Denver, Colorado. Twenty of its members in six states have been implicated in robberies of armored cars in the states of Washington and California. Members of The Order have been involved in shootouts with the FBI in Idaho, Oregon, and Washington. This group has called for revolution against minorities and the federal government.

The *Posse Comitatus* was founded in the late 1970s and is headquartered in Tigerton, Wisconsin. It opposes the federal government and the income tax. At the center of its propaganda is the claim that Jews control all of the financial institutions in the United States. In 1983 its leader was killed in a shootout with police in Arkansas after he had killed two federal agents who were trying to arrest him.

The *Aryan Brotherhood* was founded in the late 1970s and operates in prisons nationwide. Its avowed purpose is to protect white inmates. Members of the group were convicted in 1984 of killing a white guard at the federal prison in Oxford, Wisconsin.

The *Nazi Party*, founded in Germany in the 1930s, is currently active nationwide in the United States and has committed many acts of violence throughout the country, including murder. A member was recently convicted of killing two black men and a man he thought was Jewish in Cleveland, Ohio.

The *Restored Church of Jesus Christ Aryan Nation* was founded in the 1980s and is headquartered in Post Falls, Idaho. The avowed national plan of this group is to kill all blacks. Its leader was convicted of threatening a racially mixed family.

The *Christian Defense League* was founded in the early 1980s and is based in Baton Rouge, Louisiana. Its goal is to organize white Christians and "sweep the anti-Christ from our churches" and to remove Jews from public office.

The *Covenant, The Sword, and the Arm of the Lord* was founded in the 1980s and is based near the Arkansas-Missouri border. A paramilitary survivalist group operating what is called a "Christian communal settlement," it asserts that whites are descendants of Jesus and that Jews are "an anti-Christ race . . . to destroy God's people."

Coping with Hate Groups

In the early 1980s an Alabama-based organization called Klanwatch was formed to counter the violence and intimidation directed by hate groups against blacks and people who seek justice for all.

Under the aegis of the Southern Poverty Law Center (Montgomery, Alabama), Klanwatch compiles dossiers on members of the Ku Klux Klan in Georgia and throughout the country. It also tracks the movement of Klan leaders. Engaged in a multipronged approach, Klanwatch is making every effort to expose the activities of Klan members and lay the groundwork for law suits against the resurgent robed order.

Klan demonstrations, marches, and rallies—sometimes

leading to violence—are occurring more frequently in many parts of the country, and Klanwatch is attempting to document them. It has identified nearly 500 Klan members in sixteen Southern states as well as in California, Pennsylvania, Ohio, and Indiana and in Canada. According to Director Morris Dees, Klanwatch attempts to establish the rank of Klan members and to track their movements. Various methods are used to gather information, among them a service that clips Klan-related stories from 13,000 publications. The collection of Klan material from daily and weekly newspapers and magazines is augmented by photographs and videotapes of Klan activities. A videotape of Klan members attacking a group of black marchers in Decatur, Alabama, was made available to the "Phil Donahue Show" that featured Klan leader Bill Wilkinson and Georgia State Senator Julian Bond. Wilkinson is the Imperial Wizard of the militant faction of the Klan known as the Invisible Empire, Knights of the Ku Klux Klan. Bond is president of the Law Center.

Klanwatch receives strong support from political leaders who wish to serve the cause of democracy, including Senator Edward F. Kennedy:

I hope that each of you will act on this invitation from Julian Bond by giving your strong support and your contributions to the important new Klanwatch project of the Southern Poverty Law Center. I am proud of the fact that, because of my efforts, . . . the Democratic Party [has adopted] a clear and unequivocal condemnation of the Klan and its abominable activities. No American can stand silent in the face of the alarming reports and the resurgence of the Klan.

Julian Bond and the Southern Poverty Law Center have compiled an outstanding record in the fight against racism and discrimination. The effort they are now launching against the Klan deserves our vigorous support, and I urge you to join us in this cause.

Coping with hate groups is difficult: time-consuming, costly, and dangerous. It takes special methods requiring patience and skill to check the activities of these groups through legal means. The courts have to prosecute and convict those hate-group members who carry out acts of violence. Laws have to be passed to limit the freedom of hate groups to recruit youth and to disseminate terrorist propaganda. Education for democracy has to be strengthened in our schools so that each youngster learns that living in a democracy requires that the democratic rights of all must be observed and upheld.

The letter that closes this chapter gives evidence of a real person's need for organizations such as Klanwatch to protect the average citizen against terrorist activities.

Dear Mrs . . . .

I understand from my friends at the Klanwatch Project of the Southern Poverty Law Center in Montgomery that you recently sent a gift to help in their work.

I wanted to show some appreciation for the work the Center did for me and I wrote them a letter of thanks. They asked if I would share my feelings with you so that you might better understand that their work touches the lives of real people in a meaningful way. I was more than glad to help by writing you directly.

When I needed their help to protect me from harassment from members of the Ku Klux Klan, they spent hundreds of hours and several thousand dollars to protect my family and me.

Let me tell you about my case.

I am a black person living in a small rural North Carolina community and work as a guard at a state prison. I wanted to advance myself and asked my supervisor for permission to take the sergeant's examination. No black man had ever been sergeant of the prison guard.

I did not know at the time that one of the white guards was a Klansman. That night, a Klan cross was burned in the dirt road in front of my house. My wife and children were terrified. A few nights later, several Klansmen wearing sheets and paramilitary uniforms, and carrying guns, drove up in front of my home and threatened to kill me. My children were so frightened that they did not sleep well for months. Later, shots were fired at the guard tower at night from cars passing on the road.

The lawyers from the Southern Poverty Law Center's Klanwatch Project filed suit against three Klansmen suspected of this harassment. They also filed suit to stop the Carolina Knights of the KKK from operating their paramilitary army. After a few months, they received a court order stopping the Klan paramilitary training. The trial against the three Klansmen who harassed me will be held this fall.

Since the Center came to my aid, I have had no problems with the Klan and my family can once again live in peace.

You may have heard of some of the big cases the Center has handled. Many of these cases receive

national publicity and many have made significant
advances in human rights. My case is not very important in the long run and you may not ever have heard
about it, but it was important to my family and me to
be able to call on a group of lawyers who had the
money to go after the Klan and who are experts in
how to stop Klan terrorism. Funds were available to
help me only with the help from people like yourself.

The Klan is still very active in the deep South.
In small communities in Alabama, Georgia, North
Carolina and other border states, the Klan strikes fear
into the hearts of blacks who are simply trying to seek
a better way of life for their families.

For the first time in history, an organization exists
that specializes in stopping Klan violence. Until my
case, I had not heard of their work. I can assure you
that I will be one of their biggest supporters in the
future.

Please continue your financial support of the
Center. This is a long hard fight that needs people
like yourself committed to stopping violent racism.

My family and I want to personally thank you for
the generous gift that you gave the Center.

Sincerely,

BP

CHAPTER 4

The Homeless:
A New Minority

COMMUNITY UP IN ARMS AGAINST
HOMELESS SHELTER

The Community Board chairman . . . called the hearing in response to information he had received that the city planned to renege on its commitment to open a day-care center for children at the . . . site. The Community Board had approved a proposal to renovate for day-care services . . . . However, the Human Resources Administration switched its plans and decided to use the site as a homeless shelter for women.

The above news story typifies the heated discussions going on between city governments and local community boards regarding the housing of America's newest minority, the homeless. The winters of 1989 and 1990 found more Americans homeless than at any time since the dark days of the Great Depression. According to the National Coalition for the Homeless, some three million people are without homes and live on the streets entirely or find short-term housing in shelters provided by city agencies or private organizations. The U.S. Department of Housing and Urban Development (HUD) conservatively estimates the number of homeless persons at between 350,000 and 3 million nationwide. Although there is disagreement about the number, everyone agrees that it is increasing.

In New York City the problem of sheltering the homeless was thrust into the limelight when a lawsuit was filed against the city on behalf of homeless persons. The city currently finances 18 public shelters that provide nighttime beds for the thousands of homeless men and women who wander the streets during the day. About 175 churches and synagogues provide another 700 beds in 65 shelters. Funded soup kitchens that dot the metropolitan area provide hot meals for the homeless and indigent.

Who Are the Homeless?

Traditionally, the vagrants who roamed America's freight-yards and backroads, who slept on the streets of New York's Bowery or the Skid Rows of other large cities were middle-aged men, alcoholic and without family or friends. Since the early 1970s, however, the homeless population has been changing, becoming progressively younger, with an increasing number of females. A phenomenon of the 1990s is the increasing number of families, usually single women and their children, who are swelling the mass of homeless persons to a figure of more than 150,000 in New York.

Before 1970 national statistics on the homeless were not kept because no government funds were allocated

A homeless young man sleeping on a street in New York City. (Moria Joseph)

to shelter the male, mostly white, vagrant population. During the late 1960s the national policy concerning people in mental institutions changed. The process of "deinstitutionalizing" the mentally ill was put into high gear. It was found that many of the mentally ill became functional enough to care for their own basic needs when medicated with Thorazine or its family of tranquilizers. The government plan was to release psychotics from the large, state-operated mental institutions into smaller community residences where, under the supervision of a house leader, they would receive care including the psychoactive medication that would keep them nominally functional. It was reasoned that such residences would be less costly and more efficient than large institutions. Accordingly, Congress enacted a law that promised federal funding for the establishment of community-based health centers.

A law without built-in machinery for turning words into fact is no better than an unfulfilled promise. The "deinstitutionalization" law accomplished one phase of the project: reducing the population of state-controlled mental institutions. Thousands of mentally ill persons placed on temporary rations of psychoactive medication were turned away from the security of an institution to fend for themselves in communities ill equipped and ill prepared to receive them and care for them. Phase two of the deinstitutionalization plan was effected to a very minor extent in very few communities. The thousands of people turned out of mental institutions had no place to go: no housing, no mental health clinics, no support systems. They adopted the vagrant's life-style of living on the streets. Thus out of legal decree there emerged a new and pathetically vulnerable minority: a segment of society now popularly called "the homeless."

Why Homelessness?

Once released from institutions, persons who suffer from chronic mental illness lose their support system. First of all, families—who have had to bear the brunt of the unpleasantness and even the danger of coping with a person who cannot function on a level of reasonableness—remove themselves emotionally and physically from institutionalized relatives. Dealing with the mentally ill is exhausting, eroding a person's empathy, financial reserves, and patience. Local outpatient clinics, usually understaffed and underfunded, are little help to the average family of modest circumstances that is being crushed under the weight of a psychotic relative.

When a person is institutionalized over a long period, the family, thankful for relief from the burden, grows away emotionally and cannot accept the responsibility of taking the mentally ill person back into the household. If neither the family nor the government can make arrangements for the housing of a deinstitutionalized person, he or she is left to fend alone and without support. The nature of most mental illnesses is that the person cannot function on a satisfactory basis—cannot be employed, cannot respond rationally to everyday needs and situations. Therefore mentally ill persons require more watching and care than the average person or community agency can give. Persons released from mental institutions are left with no place to live: no apartment, no room.

Living on the streets represents the final state of disengagement from friends, family, and institutions that may have rendered care and protection. About 73 percent of the homeless are persons who were released from mental institutions, uncured of their illness, and left untreated in their distress. Most of these persons are loners, lacking the ability to make friends and having lost the protection of family. They are a burden and a trial, draining family financial resources without the promise of cure. The deranged personality may be difficult to deal with, having personal habits that may be repelling or even dangerous. Families cannot cope with the severely mentally disturbed.

Robert R. is thirty-nine years old, released from a mental institution where he had lived for ten years. During the time of his hospitalization, his parents died. He has two older brothers who are married and have families of their own. The brothers, as next of kin, were contacted by the social worker from the mental hospital when Robert was to be released. Neither brother could accept Robert into his home, but they made provisions for his housing and financial needs. They rented a small apartment for him and arranged for him to be put on the welfare roll as a person incapable of earning a living. For six months all went well. Then Robert slipped back into his old ways and set his apartment building on fire. The brothers refused to do any more for him. Now Robert is one of the homeless.

Mara S. had been a bookkeeper in a small firm for about fifteen years. She grew up in a small Midwestern town, which she left at the age of twenty. After moving from job to job and from town to town for about five years, she landed in New York and was employed by a small manufacturing firm. Living in a single room in an apartment hotel, she made no friends, joined no organizations, and seemed to be without family or personal ties. The hotel where she lived was sold, and the long-term tenants were required to move. Mara refused and was later evicted by court order. She quit her job, stowed her belongings into two shopping bags, and took up life on the streets. For the past five years she has been one of the "bag ladies," sleeping on the subway at night and wandering through the city with her possessions in bags.

Mara's story points out the detachment and isolation that seem to be a prequisite for homelessness. Avoidance of close personal ties with fellow humans is the personality characteristic that links those who take up the life-style of wandering the streets and seek nighttime refuge in door-ways or in cardboard boxes or other makeshift shelters.

The "New" Homeless

Not all of the homeless are dischargees from mental institutions. Swelling their ranks is a group that can be characterized as a phenomenon of modern times: homeless families. Among the homeless families are two indentifiable subgroups. First there is the unwed mother with several out-of-wedlock children. For unknown reasons these families have fallen through the cracks of the welfare system and plunged into the devastating sea of homelessness. They are usually not wanderers in the vagrant sense; rather, they are housed in temporary shelters run by church groups or other benevolent associations. Because the mothers have trouble finding and maintaining permanent housing, they remain in a given shelter as long as possible. When told to move on because the shelter is a temporary residence, they do just that—move on to another shelter. Many of these families are removed from the ranks of the homeless when assigned to a welfare hotel. Characteristically, however, something always happens that causes them to move from the hotel, and they resume their shelter-to-shelter life. Although these women have sexual contacts with males, they exhibit the overriding characteristic of isolation and detachment from family and longtime friends.

The other homeless subgroup is the family consisting of male, female, and children. These are usually on-the-road vagrants. They load an automobile with all of their belongings and move from town to town, living out of the car or van as they travel the road. Sooner or later they reach a breakdown in their life-style caused by lack of funds, lack of food, lack of the bare essentials of life. The children complicate their lives. At some point, they come to the attention of local child-abuse or welfare agencies and their plight is made known—usually publicized, rarely corrected.

Politics and the Homeless

Housing the homeless has become both a matter of politics and a matter of publicity for the vested interests. During fiscal year 1989–1990 New York City spent $300 million dollars to "house" the homeless, mostly in temporary shelters; however, little or no attention was given to their basic needs of psychiatric and medical care. Although most of the homeless are so mentally disturbed that they are beyond the help of psychiatrists, health care including regular treatment with psychoactive drugs would enable them to pursue more productive lives. The high incidence of tuberculosis and other debilitating diseases (body lice) among those who live on the streets might be lessened with care in community-based therapeutic houses and accessible health clinics.

The 1963 law that mandated the release of severely mentally disturbed persons from state mental institutions should also be used by the states to obtain funding for the housing and care of those discharged. In recent years a number of advocacy groups have come into being, supposedly to wage legal warfare over the rights of the homeless. The legal battles usually turn out to be mere skirmishes in which a coalition of advocacy groups files suit against a municipality demanding the establishment of emergency shelters. The matter of health care is not addressed.

In New York, Governor Mario Cuomo has proposed that 80,000 units of low- to middle-income housing be built in the next ten years, including 15,000 units in New York City. The number of housing units affordable to persons of low income has dwindled sharply in New York State, where housing costs and rentals have skyrocketed. Fig. 4.1 illustrates what has happened to affordable housing for low-income households. The figures are based on information gathered during a federal government's housing survey.

Increased housing for people of low income would prevent the homeless population from growing so dramatically each year. Housing units are lost to the poor through a number of tragic events. Many apartment buildings are gutted by fire; once such buildings are destroyed, they are not replaced. Owners abandon large apartment buildings, unable to make suitable profit because of the rent control laws and the inflated costs of repairs and maintenance. Abandoned buildings are condemned by the city, making the rental units unavailable to the poor. Single-room occupancy (SRO) hotels are used to house those who otherwise would be homeless; however, there are not enough SROs to meet the needs of the evergrowing homeless population.

President Reagan's observation that the "homeless are homeless because they choose to be" is an inaccurate assessment of the problem. Unemployment caused by the loss of manufacturing industries to overseas sites has the direct result of denying income to the unskilled and semiskilled worker. With no housing options available, many of the unemployed have joined the ranks of the street-living homeless.

Let us now review the several interrelated causes for homelessness: (1) loss of residency in mental institutions; (2) loss of support systems for the mentally disabled; (3) loss of housing to the poor; and (4) loss of jobs and income.

Narrowly enough, advocacy groups seem to focus on only one facet of the problem: emergency shelter for the

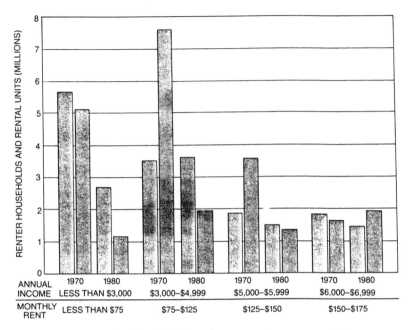

Fig. 4.1 Decrease in affordable housing over a ten-year period.

homeless. Given the fact that 80 percent of the homeless have been turned out of state mental hospitals, should lobbying groups not seek more on behalf of the homeless? Would it not be feasible to petition for the establishment of group homes and mental health centers that would provide permanent housing, health care, or ongoing support systems? Should not the more able of the homeless be trained to function in some employable capacity?

The working of politics is, indeed, strange. Politicians and political activists work to capture public attention and emotion. Speaking of $3.5 billion dollars and 15,000 housing units is more provocative than speaking of a community house that will accommodate fifteen residents and a custodian, or a health center designed to serve a local neighborhood. Although large cities need many such group

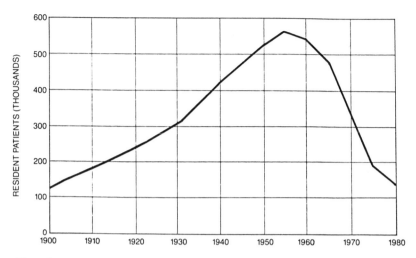

Fig. 4.2 The release of patients from mental hospitals from 1955 through 1980 decreased the number of institutionalized patients. Many of these now comprise the population of the homeless.

homes and health centers, such proposals might spell political death. Politicians want to stay in office; politics is their career and their livelihood. Political activists hope to become elected politicians or to propel themselves into the directorship of some well-funded agency. Therefore one must "keep a level head," proposing only those solutions that do not impel the voter to turn to the opposition. Politics and politicians do little to solve the very human problems of the homeless.

Communities and the Homeless

The homeless population has become highly visible on sidewalks, in the parking lots of shopping malls, in subways, in doorways, anywhere that protects from the winter wind and shades from the summer sun. That high visibility has caused some communities to react against this wandering horde of vagrants who formerly stayed put in Skid Row.

Middle-income homeowners usually have invested a lifetime of work and savings in a modest house in a quiet neighborhood. They do not want to share the community for which they have struggled with those unsightly persons whose presence can only serve to bring down property values. With the help of local community boards, organizations of homeowners have formed to prevent the invasion of their neighborhoods by scores of homeless. A case in point: Two churches in a section of Brooklyn, New York, applied for permits to give temporary shelter to ten homeless persons (five for each church). When news of the applications reached the local community board, board members helped to fan the flames of community ire. Hastily formed "Save the community" groups demanded that the churches rescind the applications and desist from activities that might bring the homeless into the neighborhood. Another case: When a former YWCA, also in Brooklyn, was to be converted into a shelter for homeless women, the community board used all legal means to defeat the plan. In another locality, a large house was burned to the ground because it was to be used as a group home for mentally retarded young adults.

Shelters and soup kitchens operate successfully in nonresidential sections of cities where the coming and going of vagrants does not infringe on the rights and esthetic sensibilities of home owners. Churches on the periphery of localities that are dotted with abandoned factories and apartment buildings are best able to attend to the homeless. City shelters with their barracks-like sleeping quarters meet little opposition when established in areas of deteriorating housing and nonresidential buildings.

Community and advocacy groups could best serve the homeless by joining forces to demand better care for

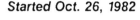

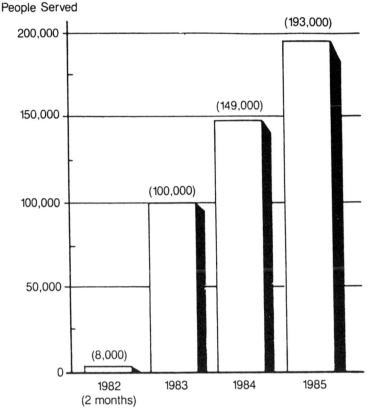

Fig. 4.3 The increase in numbers of persons served by a church-sponsored soup kitchen in New York City.

them. They should be cleaned up, properly clothed and housed, and given health care and medication to enable them to respond more acceptably to society.

In New York City the shelters for homeless men are dangerous, dirty, and inadequate for healthy living. The numbers of homeless men are so great that huge barracks-type buildings are used to house from 250 to 500 men per night. About 80 percent of those using the shelters are

addicted to drugs or alcohol. Their behavior is that of
addicts: unstable and violent. It is not unusual for for
sleeping residents to be robbed or physically attacked.
Therefore, many homeless persons feel safer sleeping on
the streets than in city-run shelters.

The situation for women is also difficult. Most homeless
women who have children are sheltered in church facilities
or in welfare hotels.

Homeless adults cope by adopting behavioral patterns
that permit them to live a life on the streets. But what
of homeless families? What happens to children who
wander as nomads from shelter to shelter? Who should
take responsibility for the children?

CHAPTER 5

The Impoverished Black Family

The Erosion of Family Life

In poor black communities it is quite evident that family life has disintegrated. The breakdown of the traditional family structure has reached such proportions that social scientists say it threatens to erode the economic gains made by blacks. The marks of the disintegrating family—a phenomenon that has developed since the 1960s—are as follows: Nearly half of all black households are headed by women, a rapidly increasing proportion, and more than 50 percent of black babies are born to unwed mothers. The fact that 70 percent of black children come from homes where a single female heads the household accounts for the increased poverty into which black children have slipped. In a recent study, the Children's Defense Fund found that, compared to white children, black children are twice as likely to:

- Die in the first year of life;
- Be born prematurely;
- Suffer low birth weight;
- Have a mother who received late or no prenatal care;
- Be born to a teenage or single-parent family;
- Live in substandard housing;
- Be suspended from school or suffer corporal punishment;
- Be unemployed as teenagers;
- Have no parent employed;
- Live in an institution.

They are three times as likely to:

- Be poor;
- Have their mother die in childbirth;
- Live with a parent separated from a spouse;
- Live in a female-headed family;
- Be murdered between five and nine years of age;
- Be in foster care;
- Die of known child abuse.

Four times as likely to:

- Live with neither parent and be supervised by a child welfare agency;
- Be murdered before one year of age or as a teenager;
- Be jailed between fifteen and nineteen years of age.

Five times as likely to:

- Be dependent on welfare;
- Become pregnant as a teenager.

Twelve times as likely to:

• Live with a parent who never married.

Currently forums sponsored by such organizations as the National Urban League and the National Association for the Advancement of Colored People are being held in major cities throughout the United States to address the problem of family disintegration in the black ghettos. The planners of the forums reject the idea that the black family is inherently unstable and cite major changes in the economic structure of the country that have made poor blacks poorer.

The Problem Defined

Scholars and politicians have attributed the breakdown of the poor black family to a number of job-related and societal factors that have surfaced since World War II. Since 1960 the job market has just about dried up for black males. The Center for the Study of Social Policy in Washington reports that since 1960 the number of black males over the age of eighteen has doubled, but the number of employed has drastically declined.

The loss of jobs is directly related to changes in the job markets in the rural South and the industrial centers of Northern cities. In the South, traditionally, large numbers of farm hands, unskilled workers, were needed on the cotton, tobacco, and produce farms. Mechanization of the farms decreased that need, and displaced farm laborers left the South in years prior to World War II and even into the 1950s, flocking to Northern cities seeking jobs in

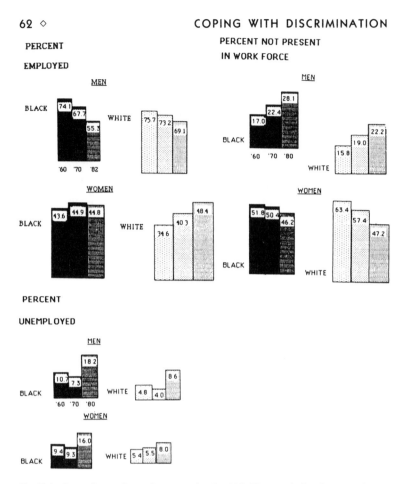

Fig. 5.1 Overview of employment in the U.S. The statistics from which these graphs were drawn indicate a serious income gap between blacks and whites.

the factories and relief from unemployment. While the factories operated at full capacity, they were able to absorb huge numbers of unskilled and semiskilled laborers.

Beginning in the 1960s, however, the job markets in the North began to change. As more and more manufacturing was moved to countries overseas where labor is cheap, the factories either closed or maintained minimal operations.

As factories closed, so did job opportunities for black men. Thus the poor black male has found himself displaced as a farm laborer and shut out of jobs in industrialized centers.

The graphs in Figure 5.1 show the percentage of employment for blacks and whites over a period of twenty-two years. Each graph shows the dramatic decline in the number of black people in the American labor force. The statistics, prepared by the Bureau of Labor Statistics, confirm that job loss to black men has been more than twice that of white men.

Although white women entered the labor market in the years following 1960, their rate of unemployment in 1988 was only half that of black women. These statistics indicate that blacks lag far behind whites in employment, and the gap grows ever greater.

Prior to 1948, before the erosion of rural farm-labor jobs and unskilled factory jobs, black male employment was 87 percent, almost a full point higher than that of white males. Although the jobs held by blacks were menial and low-paying, they constituted the male as a steady wage earner and established him as head of the household. Chronic unemployment among black males has led to the breakdown of family life of the poor.

The Effects of Chronic Unemployment

A woman petitioning family court for the custody of her four grandnephews expressed herself thus:

> My two brothers, my nephew, my nieces were all beaten by the system. Now I am trying to do something for these four little grandnephews of mine. Perhaps they can overcome the system and have successful lives.

The "system" spoken of by the petitioner is more pre-
cisely known as "institutional racism." Racism that denies
the impoverished black person a fair share of American
opportunity is woven into the fabric of every institution
that touches his life. That institution might be the labor
union that denies him full membership or even admittance
to an apprentice program. It might be the steel mill or
other industrial plant in which the black man is the last
hired and the first fired. The denying institution might be
a social service agency such as the welfare system, which
breaks up black families by withholding aid to families in
which the husband is present. It might be the landlord
who overcharges for substandard housing, or the ghetto
school that has lost its effectiveness. Whatever the institution, the outcome is the same for the poor black person: It
makes him more impoverished.

Chronic unemployment and denial changes the psyche
of people. This changed psyche is evident in the masses of
unemployed black males who inhabit the urban ghettos,
where another life-style has developed. This new life-style,
which is for the most part antisocial, involves cunning,
crime, and ways of making underground money. Much
illegal money passes through the ghetto in drug sales,
illegal bookmaking, numbers running, pimping, and prostitution. That underground money remains in the hands
of a very few successful "entrepreneurs." The large mass of
ghetto inhabitants become more devastated: drug addicted, schizophrenic, imprisoned for crimes committed.

The ghetto looms larger than the blighted areas of de-
cayed and burned-out housing. The ghetto is a way of life
with a beat of its own, outside the mainstream of American
life. Its streets are dominated by unemployed black males,
who, having lost their role as wage earner, use up their life
in fitful idleness that culminates in violence against one

another, their family, or those in the mainstream society. A recent study of the prison population made by the Justice Department found that black men are nearly six times as likely as whites to serve time in state prison. Over a lifetime, between 11.6 and 18.7 percent of black men can be expected to serve a sentence in an adult state prison, compared with from 2.1 to 3.3 percent of white males.

Ghetto life is not conducive to stable family life, which requires a healthy breadwinning male at the helm. Impoverished blacks are removed from their role as family head by imprisonment, by being disabled by drugs, or by assuming a destructive personal philosophy that cripples them psychologically. Without opportunities for employment, without hope for the future, the black male sinks in a morass of poverty. He becomes economically emasculated and is deemed worthless by society. In direct reaction to the pervasive economic deprivation, the male attempts to flaunt his manhood in other ways: the "ditty-bop" walk so characteristic of ghetto blacks, the siring of innumerable out-of-wedlock children, and toughness and violence.

The Department of Health and Human Services in a recent report concluded that black, Hispanic, and native American people die younger and are generally less healthy than non-Hispanic whites. The grim statistics reveal that there were 18,000 more deaths each year among blacks from heart disease and stroke than would occur if their health were on a par with that of whites. Also among blacks, there were 11,000 excess deaths from homicides and accidents, 8,100 excess deaths from cancer, 6,100 from infant mortality, 2,150 from cirrhosis of the liver, and 1,850 from diabetes. These six health areas account for more than 80 percent of the total disparity in health status between the black and white populations.

The rate of death from cancer in the black population is

considered quite serious. The death rate from lung cancer
is 45 percent higher among black men than among white
men. From cancer of the esophagus, the death rate for
black men is three times that of white men. Black men die
of prostate cancer at twice the rate of white men. The
mortality rate among black women from cancer of the
cervix is about two and a half times that of white women.

Added to these statistics are the following: Black males
under the age of forty-five are ten times more likely to die
from hypertension than white males. Coronary heart
disease rates are twice as high in black women as in white
women. The statistics for black children raised in the
ghetto given at the beginning of this chapter show that
these children are born into hard circumstances that do
not change for the better in their lifetime. To say the least,
life as a ghetto black is grim and forbidding.

Coping with Poverty

Poverty and its concomitant life-style in the ghetto have
developed an underclass of people who are without resources and without hope, existing at the edge of society.
One generation produces another of like kind, perpetu-
ating a cycle of unemployment, out-of-wedlock births,
welfare recipients, juvenile delinquents and adult crim-
inals, and households headed by single women. This cycle
of relentless poverty and hopelessness must be broken.

Black men and women who have escaped the ghetto
through education and its ensuing opportunities have
moved into the affluent suburbs just like their white counterparts. As the economically more able blacks move away
from the decaying urban communities, those left behind

become more deeply enmeshed in socially unacceptable patterns of living.

Stirred into action by the worsening conditions in the ghetto and having had their consciousness raised by a White House Conference report made in the mid-1960s, the black middle class is now focusing its attention on the poor black family. In 1966 Daniel Patrick Moynihan, then Assistant Secretary of Labor, prepared a report titled, "The Negro Family: The Case for National Action." At that time black leaders were totally absorbed with the problems of segregation and felt that the publishing of the report would hurt the cause of integration.

Two decades later, the report has been accepted because the plight of the ghetto black can no longer be ignored. An affluent black sorority, Delta Sigma Theta, has taken up the issue of the black family as a special project for its chapters across the country. The National Association for the Advancement of Colored People and the National Urban League are addressing the problem of the black family, seeking ways to break the cycle of impoverishment and crime.

In a *New York Times Magazine* article, "Restoring the Traditional Black Family," Eleanor Holmes Norton proposes that the many problems of the black family have to be identified and studied in their entirety. Tackling one problem and allowing the others to fester compounds the sickness in the ghetto. Mrs. Norton suggests that a significant step in breaking the cycle of idleness and its accompanying antisocial behavior is *prevention*. Through programs devised to carry the participants through a series of graded steps in a disciplined process, the poor can be weaned from public assistance and helped to gain independence. Programs that help prevent teenage pregnancy, job training for boys and young men, and counseling that will help reshape attitudes in the young can be made the core of an action program that will indeed be of immediate benefit to the impoverished black.

The Role of the Federal Government

The United States government must accept the major responsibility for alleviating the chronic unemployment of the black male, for providing health services for the impoverished, and for instituting educational programs to broaden the horizons of those living in the ghetto. Under the administration of President Ronald Reagan programs designed to help the poor were eradicated, leaving those most in need worse off than ever. For example, aid to poor children in the form of subsidized school lunches has been reduced. Not only is it more difficult for a poor child to qualify for free school lunch, but also the amount of protein in the lunch has been decreased. This circumstance is a disgrace for a country that grows so much food that it is given away to other countries or destroyed. The Reagan administration was insensitive to the basic needs of the poor. While emphasizing the philosophy of "self help," the Reagan administration urged Congress to cut back spending for Medicaid, community health centers, family planning, and other public health programs.

A committee of five Roman Catholic bishops has released a document titled, "Pastoral Letter on Catholic Social Teaching and the U.S. Economy," which calls for a new effort to aid the poor. The letter denounces the existence of widespread poverty in the midst of American plenty as "a social and moral scandal that must not be ignored." Underscored is the fact that 14.4 percent of the U.S. population lives below the official poverty line,

which, for a family of four, is set at an annual income of
$10,000. The bishops insist that the federal government
must do more to reduce unemployment. They call the
present rate of joblessness "morally unacceptable" and
urge the government to take direct action in providing
training programs to make the unemployable useful in the
labor market.

Recently, the New York State Social Services Commission announced a new system in which more than
220,000 employable welfare recipients would be required
to work or to enroll in job training and educational programs. The plan differs from others in that it stresses
placing recipients in career-oriented jobs rather than
having them work in unskilled jobs only to earn welfare
benefits. The Department of Labor would refer welfare
clients to both public and private jobs. In a job with a
private business, the welfare system may pay part of the
recipient's salary for up to six months, at which time he or
she would either become a permanent employee of the
company or be referred to another job. Ann Montalbano
of the American Public Welfare Association has described
the plan as "one of the more comprehensive efforts" under-
taken by a state.

Blacks Need Help

This chapter has shown that black unemployment and its
concomitant poverty remain unacceptably high. The social
and psychological destruction that results from chronic
unemployment will not remain isolated in the ghetto
areas of the cities but will spill over and infect the mainstream society. It must be realized that the working middle
class are being pushed into poverty by the tax burden
imposed on them to support welfare, prisons, walk-in

health facilities—all being overused by the burgeoning population of unemployed black males. More alarming is the new generation of poor children that are living in greater poverty than ever in the history of the United States. About 13.8 million (22 percent) of Americans under the age of 18 live in poverty; in 1969 the percentage was 14.3. Forty-eight percent of all black children currently live in poverty, as compared to 39.6 percent in 1969. Although the number of the elderly poor has increased, government spending on programs for children has decreased, causing poor children to be poorer. The major source of this problem is the emergence of single-parent families. It is estimated that in the 1990s about half the children coming of age will have lived in a one-parent family. A third of the children born—one half in New York City—will spend part of their life on welfare. The vast majority of black children born in poverty tend to remain poor throughout their lives.

To help families climb out of poverty, the government must take direct action. The critical needs are for effective education, job training, and family support. The new work plan adopted by New York State to help welfare recipients join the ranks of the responsible working class is a step in the right direction. Affirmative action plans need to be revived and strengthened so that qualified black young people can have the doors of private industry opened to them.

In addition to the efforts of local and federal governments, responsible black community groups and organizations must take a firm hand in the education of black youth. The education of the black male requires special attention. In the black community one out of twenty-one black males is murdered each year by other black males. Drugs and jail destroy the lives of others. Educational awareness has to

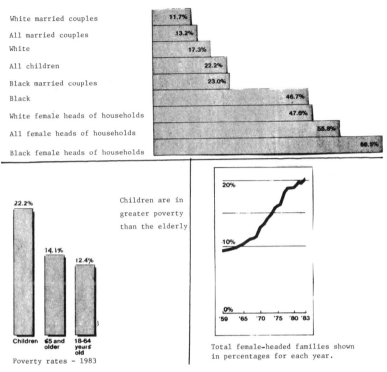

White married couples — 11.7%
All married couples — 13.2%
White — 17.3%
All children — 22.2%
Black married couples — 23.0%
Black — 46.7%
White female heads of households — 47.6%
All female heads of households — 55.8%
Black female heads of households — 66.9%

22.2%   14.1%   12.4%

Children   65 and older   18-64 years old
Poverty rates – 1983

Children are in greater poverty than the elderly

20%

10%

0%
'59   '65   '70   '75   '80 '83

Total female-headed families shown in percentages for each year.

Fig. 5.2. It is customary to excuse the failure of vast numbers of black men to support their children by citing their difficulty in finding employment. The National Urban League indicates that the divorce rate among blacks quadrupled between 1960 and 1990 and that permanent separation is nearly as common as divorce. More than half of all women raising children alone receive no financial support from the fathers. More than 13 million children are officially poor. A family headed by a woman is 4½ times more likely to be poor than one headed by a man.

be heightened in the inner-city black family. Education and self-determination must replace crime, drugs, and out-of-wedlock births.

CHAPTER 6

Women's Issues

Sexism is alive. It's alive in the United Nations, it's alive in the U.S. Government—and it's bipartisan. [But sexism is] not unconquerable, if one can only avoid getting angry and wasting one's energy on rage.
—Jeanne J. Kirkpatrick,
former Chief U.S. Delegate to the United Nations

The Feminist Point of View

New words are always being added to our language; old ones are often revived. *Feminist* is a "new-old" word that has become a useful adjunct to our modern vocabulary and thinking. A word in itself is useless without the solid base of meaningful philosophy or dynamic imagery that gives it substance. The word feminist is a powerful one including both concept and description.

In concept, "feminism" is a strong belief in the rights of women and in their worth as human beings entitled to the full rights of citizenship and unbiased protection of the law. Feminist is also descriptive of a woman who is dedicated to working on behalf of women's causes. Identifying the issues of women's rights and working to address women's concerns are the goals of the feminist movement.

The idea of feminism is not new. In the July 4, 1985, issue of *New York Newsday*, Francine Prose told a story illustrating the spunk of some members of the New York State Woman Suffrage Association. When the Statue of Liberty was formally unveiled in October, 1866, women were barred from the ceremony on grounds that their "delicate constitutions" might be endangered by stampeding crowds. The suffragettes were not to be denied; they hired their own boat from which they not only viewed the ceremony, but also made speeches of their own. They were delighted that Liberty had been personified as a woman but were offended that a metal sculpture was given greater respect than living women.

To the disadvantage of modern women, this "double think" in assessing their worth and strength still persists. For example, the concept of motherhood in the United States is held in high esteem, glorified—so much so that special-interest groups have taken it upon themselves to destroy abortion clinics by bombing them or by harassing their patients. Yet, once motherhood becomes an established fact, women who are heads of households are denied legislation that could remove them from a chronic state of poverty.

In 1966 Betty Friedan founded the National Organization for Women (NOW), an organization dedicated to focusing national attention on women's rights and their role in society. This began the modern feminist movement. With many politically active chapters throughout the United States, NOW has been responsible for raising the consciousness level in thinking about women and has brought sharply into public focus the issues that affect women: poverty, politics, family violence, education, equal pay for equal work, equal employment opportunities, women athletes, and even a new look at the psychology of women. Many other organizations now work on behalf of women, and the women's movement has spread to other countries. The feminist movement has begun to change the way men think about women and the way women think about themselves.

Psychology Takes a New Look at Women

Psychology is revising its view of women. The traditional theories were developed by male psychologists, who merely measured the psychological aspects of women against the yardstick of male drives and behavior. Women psychologists are now carrying out extensive research to remove sex bias from theories of psychology. The intent is to revise mainstream theory to eliminate discrimination between the sexes in the search for social equality and justice. Sigmund Freud called women's psychology a "dark continent," and psychologist R. Lawrence Kohlberg assesses women's moral development as "stunted."

To correct the faulty conclusions of the past, a number of competent women researchers in psychology and psychoanalytic theory are finding out about women. Dr. Carol Tavris, a social psychologist, carried out a survey of 10,000 women between the ages of seventeen and thirty for *Mademoiselle* magazine. Only 2 percent of the women polled did not expect to work after marriage, whereas half planned to earn over $25,000 per year. Drs. Grace Baruch and Rosalind Barnett of Wellesley College found that motherhood was a main source of distress, while working was a key to well-being of women. Contrary to the stereotype of the happy homemaker, women with children who did not work were more unhappy than women with children who did work.

According to Dr. Baruch, ". . . the greatest sense of well-being is among women who have high-level jobs, are mothers, and are married. Juggling these multiple roles does not stress women. Work seems to be a buffer against the stresses of motherhood because it offers a sense of mastery of a sort that raising children does not." The quality of life for the woman with education and with life goals that combine career and family is far superior to that of the undereducated woman who seeks to raise a family by herself.

The new feminist psychology is also examining the way in which the sexes learn. Drs. Carol Jacklin and Eleanor Maccoby are studying hundreds of children in Los Angeles trying to sort out the sex differences that affect learning. Initial results indicate that among children entering school, girls are verbally brighter and boys are more aggressive. Further studies are being conducted to determine whether these and other differences between the sexes are learned or inherited.

Dr. Carol Gilligan, a psychologist at Harvard University, is looking into the nurturing quality of women that gives them a different outlook on life from that of men. Another study is examining the expectations of women as to companionship and intimacy in an effort to sort out the components of modern American loneliness.

Poverty and Women

The picture painted by feminist psychologists of the happy educated woman balancing career and family with equal skill does not apply to the greater percentage of American women and their children. For a large segment of this

country's women, life is not upbeat and happy or even
career-wise productive, because they are slipping back-
ward into a morass of poverty. Dr. Diana Pearce, who first
signaled the trend toward impoverished women, called
this the "feminization of poverty."

Statistics reveal that between 1978 and 1988 the number
of impoverished women who headed households rose by
150,000 each year. During the following years women
and children bore the brunt of federal budget cuts that
increased the number of poor in the United States by
30 percent.

A report titled "Inequality of Sacrifice" has been published by civil rights, education, labor, religious, and
women's organizations, including the National Organization for Women, the League of Women Voters, the
American Nurses Association, the Older Women's League,
the Children's Defense Fund, the United Methodist
Church, and the Girls Clubs of America. The report cites
the effects of "Reaganomics" on poor women and their
dependent children. Cuts in aid to dependent children,
food stamps, food supplements, school lunch subsidies,
and Medicaid have driven already impoverished families
deeper into poverty. The plan to abolish the Legal Services
Corporation, whose clients are mainly women, and the
repeal of the family planning program under the Public
Health Service Act will deprive poor women of further
important support services.

Organizations working on behalf of the female poor point
out a serious consequence of decreasing aid to needy
families and thus pushing them deeper into poverty.
Unrelenting poverty creates a class of female poor who out
of desperation will work for exploitative wages under
substandard conditions of health and safety and without
health insurance and pension benefits.

Coping with poverty can drive women heads of households into illegal acts such as working "off the books" or becoming involved in illicit enterprises. It also increases alcoholism.

The Work World and Women

Getting women out of poverty while preventing others from slipping into it is a major challenge for feminist activists. An organization called Non-Traditional Employment for Women works actively to get women into construction jobs as unskilled laborers. Such jobs in New York City pay $15.00 per hour, which a quite different from $3.85 per hour minimum wage paid in unskilled jobs designated for women. Women who apply to enter the construction field as trainees are usually poor and heads of households, subsisting on a minimum welfare allowance. On a large construction site, fewer than one percent of the workers are women. Organizations that fight for women's work rights petition for affirmative action through the United States Equal Employment Opportunity Commission and the state Human Rights Division.

The battle for women's rights in the workplace has to be fought through legislative channels. The Congressional Caucus for Women, established in 1977, has been instrumental in drawing up and introducing legislation of benefit to women. For example, the Economic Equity Act of 1985 consists of twenty-two pieces of legislation designed to remove discriminatory practices from issues concerning women. Among this legislation are bills that deal with pay equity, nondiscriminatory insurance, improved pensions for military spouses, and child care in public housing. Of primary importance is the Civil Rights Restoration Act, a bill designed to restore the full effect of the legislation

Dualism about women's roles in the workplace has always existed. A
woman worker in the garment trades in New York City at the turn of
the century was treated as harshly as a male worker (International
Ladies Garment Workers Union).

that prohibits sex discrimination at institutions receiving federal aid.

The Caucus consists of 125 men and 15 women Senators and members of the House of Representatives, reflecting the small number of legislative women. The group works on consensus, avoiding issues that are divisive. During the 1983–84 legislative year, it succeeded in getting passed ten major pieces of legislation, including pension reform for women and child-support enforcement.

Equitable treatment of women in the work world will be made possible only through strong legislation action. Recently a major manufacturer of electrical appliances was fined $8 million dollars for denying 2,000 women opportunities for equal employment and promotion. Represented by a woman attorney, the women who shared in the settlement had at least thirty years of service with the company that treated them as second-class citizens.

Currently, the average American working woman earns 62 cents for every dollar earned by a man. Although the law stipulates that equal pay must be given for equal work, the gap in salary between women and men remains. Women's groups attribute the wage disparity to the fact that lower-paying jobs are classified as women's work. To correct the wage gap, the concept of "comparable worth" was proposed. Explained by Eleanor Holmes Norton, former head of the Equal Employment Opportunity Commission, "Women are doing valuable work which just happens to be underpaid because it is done by women."

In theory, the concept of comparable worth aims to measure the intrinsic value of different jobs—that is, to compare what a typist does with what a truck driver does—and to arrive at a numerical figure (salary base) for each. An example is the Rockford (Illinois) Housing Authority; the administrative staff was 85 percent female and the maintenance staff was 85 percent male, but the males received higher wages.

Those who oppose the idea of comparable worth claim that women's own choices, social norms, and the labor market concentrate women in 20 out of the 427 categories identified by the Department of Labor.

Women's groups view the low pay of jobs predominantly held by women as discriminatory and exploitative and have actively sought change. However, in a recent ruling the Equal Employment Opportunity Commission dismissed "comparable worth" as a way to combat wage discrimination. The Commission stated that it would be impossible to take on wholesale restructuring of wages that were set by non-sex-based decisions of employers, by collective bargaining in the marketplace. Groups in favor of the comparable worth idea have vowed not to let it die, although the Reagan administration had launched an all-out attack on the concept.

Not all women in the workforce are in low-paying jobs. Liz Roman Gallese, a business journalist, in 1985 made a study of what happened to sixteen women who in 1975 had graduated from Harvard Business School with the degree of MBA. She found that all but eight of the women were working full time; five had part-time jobs, and the remaining three were planning to return to work. The majority were working for banks, insurance companies, or real estate firms. Fourteen were consultants, and six were entrepreneurs. Most were earning high salaries and had impressive titles. Mrs. Gallese found that "those women who were ambitious for their careers were just as likely to be married and to have children as to be single or divorced." The women who do want children and have them seem able to raise a family and climb the career ladder also. Education and personal ambition make it

Sally J. Ride, first American woman astronaut.

possible for women to become upwardly mobile in the world of business.

Women in Science

Women comprise nearly 50 percent of the American work-force, yet only 6 percent are employed as research or teaching scientists or engineers. The fact that so few women pursue science careers is worrisome to some observers. Research by Dr. Jane Butler Kahle of Purdue University and her graduate students among high school and college females revealed some interesting facts. First of all, the research team found that girls in the age range of thirteen to seventeen years have very negative attitudes toward science study, which reflect societal attitudes toward women in science. Parents do not value achievement in science by their daughters, while teachers seek excellence in males.

Because of the societal negative attitudes, high school girls and college women take fewer science and mathematics courses than their male counterparts and tend to score lower than men on science aptitude tests. Also the absence of role models influences girls to perceive the study of physics, chemistry, and geology as masculine. Thus societal biases and education deficits keep the numbers of females in science careers unusually small in our technological country.

For those women who are scientists, the job market and promotion opportunities are very slim. Recently, the Sloan Foundation awarded grants to ninety young scientists, only six of whom were women. James D. Koerner, vice president of the foundation, attributed the fact that only 7 percent of the awards were granted to women to the fact that women are not well represented in most scientific disciplines. A better assessment is that women are inadequately represented among young tenure-track science faculties engaged in major research. Dr. Rosalyn S. Yalow, the only American-trained woman ever to win a Nobel Prize, was the first women to be hired by the physics department of the University of Illinois. Dr. Yalow asserts that there is still discrimination against women scientists.

She, however, is a top-notch scientist who got her start during World War II when there was a shortage of male competitors.

Judith Franz, chairman of the Committee on the Status of Women of the American Physical Society, and Lilli Hornig, of the National Academy of Science Committee on the Education and Employment of Women in Science and Engineering, cite statistics that show marked differences in salaries, hiring, and rates of unemployment and promotion between women and men scientists. Salary differences range from 15 to 20 percent in most science disciplines. In chemistry, the salary differences between women and men are up to 28 percent. Chemistry is the most biased of all of the science positions; there are almost no women in leading chemistry departments. In research universities, very few women hold tenure-track positions anywhere. Women in science are not promoted as often or as fast as men.

It is also true that women scientists receive less recognition for their work than do men. A glaring example is the work done by Rosalind Franklin in the discovery of DNA, the molecule of heredity. The accolades and the Nobel Prize went to Francis Crick and James D. Watson. Dr. Franklin was given no recognition.

Among university hiring practices in the 1980s, only 12 out of 364 tenured faculty members at Harvard are women, a figure that represents 3 percent of the total. At the University of Pennsylvania, 81 of the 965 tenured faculty are women (8.5 percent), and at Princeton only 10 of the 390 tenured professors are female (2.5 percent).

The Minnesota Mining and Manufacturing Company is acting to ease the nationwide shortage of women in science. To interest young females in considering a career in chemistry, the company sends out teams of women scientists to high schools and colleges to present career guidance talks. The company has also helped form a consortium of five colleges in which programs have been developed to stimulate more interest in chemistry among undergraduates. Of special interest are women students who might go on to earn doctorates.

The efforts of private industry to encourage women to pursue careers in science is commendable. However, the education of more women scientists must be followed by equity in jobs, salary, opportunities for promotion, and recognition for work well done.

During a recent symposium on women and their health, Nobel laureate Yalow summed up women's struggle up the ladder of achievement: "Discrimination has kept many women from high places in politics, science, and other fields. We cannot expect in the immediate future that those who will seek it will achieve equality of opportunity, but if women are to start moving towards that goal, we must believe in ourselves or no one else will believe in us. The world cannot afford the loss of half its people if we are to solve the problems that beset us."

No matter the difficulty in seeking equality of opportunity, women must keep striving. The educated woman, the woman with graduate training in science and technology, will at some point in history compete successfully with her male counterpart.

SCORECARD OF GLOBAL VIOLENCE AGAINST WOMEN

In the United States, one in eight movies released commercially depicts acts of violence against women.
In the Sudan, 94 percent of all women are illiterate.

In Kuwait, women are denied the right to vote.

In Iran, the fundamentalist Islamic interpretation of the Koran makes it illegal to execute a woman who is virgin. Therefore, virgin women sentenced to death for an infraction of Islamic rules are raped before execution.

In Thailand, the work of 41.5 percent of all women working in the Bangkok area is prostitution. Seventy percent of Thai prostitutes are infected with venereal disease.

In Pakistan, the evidence of two women equals that of one man in the application of certain laws.

In Brazil, a husband can murder his wife, plead suspicion of infidelity, and then be set free with any proof of the alleged infidelity.

In India, 50 percent of the women gain no weight during the third trimester of pregnancy due to near-starvation diet.

In the Soviet Union, the average woman has approximately 12 abortions because contraceptives, although legal, are hard to obtain.

In Latin America, approximately 40 percent of maternal deaths are caused by improperly performed illegal abortions.

In South Africa, violence against black women by black men is common. Black women are beaten up so routinely on the streets that no one pays attention to the violence.

In the United States, a woman is battered every 18 seconds; raped every 3 seconds.

In Java, 80 percent of the pregnant and nursing mothers are anemic.

In Africa and on the Arabian peninsula, girls at puberty are genitally mutilated by clitoridectomy. It is estimated that 70,000,000 alive today have been subjected to this barbaric surgery.

In China, the killing of female babies has increased. The government has decreed that each couple may have only one child. The traditional preference for sons has created an epidemic of drownings and other murders of girl babies.

Violence Against Women

The preceding "Scorecard" clearly illustrates why violence against women has become an issue of urgent concern to women's groups and those who seek justice for women. Acts of violence against women are global. In the United States special-interest groups are taking action to protect women from ever-increasing brutality. ·

Films and television have done much to glorify sexual violence against women. Psychologist Edward Donnerstein of the University of Wisconsin assessed the psychological effects on men who watched a series of movies featuring graphic scenes of violence to young women. The subjects were given psychological tests before and after viewing a set of "slasher" type movies. After several viewings, they found the movies to be progressively less upsetting and more enjoyable and considered them less debasing to women.

The Donnerstein study and others of its kind reveal that the more scenes of violence against women are watched by men, the more acceptable the violence becomes. Movies that portray cruelty to women reinforce the notion that brutality is an acceptable mode of behavior.

Psychologists believe that power is at the root of violence. Violence is the misuse of power. Psychological studies of rapists have shown that most are sexually stimulated by one or more nonsex aspects of rape: subjugation, degradation, or domination of women. Rape is a brutal assault on a woman and cannot be considered merely as sexual intercourse. Rapists are men with severe personality disorders who are aroused by the fantasy of violence to women. However, while mental derangement is an important factor in rape, the overall *climate of attitudes* toward women is also a very important factor. To a large extent, the visual media help shape attitudes in the viewing public. Although rape is an abnormal expression of power, movie portrayals have made this brutality appear to be normal male behavior.

Men who exert violence against women need therapy and psychological counseling. A group called EMERGE, a male collective that works with abusive men, suggests that violence is an extreme means of control. Abusive men, whether rapist, batterer, or sexual harasser, can be likened to members of terrorist groups—their control and power are bolstered by fear of violence created in women. As long as women exist in a state of terror, abusive men feel greater power.

As borne out by statistics, sexual violence against women is becoming common. Perhaps it seems more common because women are no longer hiding acts of brutality perpetrated against them, but are seeking public redress. However, when violence against women is reduced to numbers, they are staggering. One woman in three will be raped by a stranger. One out of two women will be sexually abused before the age of eighteen, usually by a family member or a close friend of the family. One woman is seven will be raped by her husband. Women and children are more likely to experience sexual and physical violence than are men.

Battering, the beating of women by their husbands or

men with whom they are associated, is classified as addictive behavior. Men who batter their wives or girlfriends often promise to stop and do stop for a short time, but then they begin the battering again, each successive episode becoming worse than the one before. To protect women from a battering mate, shelters have been set up in cities across the nation. Psychologists are beginning to study the behavior of women housed in the shelters, identifying some common characteristics. It seems that women who remain in violent relationships become abnormally helpless and dependent. Some of them even walk away from the shelter with the man who has been beating them and believe that they are responsible for his violent behavior. Most of these women try to control their children through violence.

Prevention of Battering

There are no accurate statistics on the true extent of battered women, but known cases give evidence of the seriousness of the problem. Recently the U.S. Department of Health and Human Services prepared a study, *Family Violence*, indicating that wife battering occurs in 1.8 million couples; it is believed, however, that this study reveals only the tip of the iceberg.

Women themselves must take steps to prevent battering or, once started, to stop it. Let us turn our attention first to its prevention. Women must exercise increased awareness to detect a potential wife beater before marriage. The checklist that follows may be helpful.

Does the man:
_____ have a poor self-image?
_____ exhibit angry outbursts?

_____ become argumentative over minor issues?

_____ punch and kick walls and furniture when angered?

_____ come from a violent home?

_____ change jobs frequently?

_____ exhibit fits of jealousy?

_____ drink excessively or use other drugs?

_____ own or display a gun, knife, or other lethal weapon?

A woman contemplating marriage to a man with the above characteristics should reconsider her involvement. Another indicator of a potential batterer is one who initially engages in playful slaps and horseplay. As tension mounts, the slaps become real hits and punches during episodes of rage that end in violence. During the "cooling off" period the batterer proclaims that he is sorry for his behavior and becomes quite loving. However, the pattern recurs.

Once the first episode of battering occurs, what should the woman do? Until recently, the police held to the adage, "Never create a police problem where only a family problem exists." Thus they ignored entreaties for help from battered wives. Now, in most large cities, the police are required to provide immediate protection to a woman who seeks help. If they fail to do so, individual police officers can be brought up on charges of negligence. In New York City, a trained crisis-intervention unit handles cases of family violence.

The courts have often been unfair to battered women who have fought back against the brutality of their husbands. In most instances the courts are reluctant to handle assault cases in which the woman wants to press charges against her physically abusive husband. Roadblocks such as payment to lawyers, the requirement of two witnesses to the assault, or the assertion that the "husband may lose his job if you file a suit against him" are devices used to discourage women from availing themselves of the protection of the law. Women have killed their violent husband in an act of self-defense while being beaten and have been sentenced to prison terms. Attorney Barbara Swartz, a New York University law professor and a specialist on women in prisons, states that our prisons house hundreds of women who finally fought back after years of beatings, rape, and other forms of violence.

Women's groups, community agencies, society as a whole, and battered women themselves have begun to raise public consciousness about the violence that goes on behind closed doors. With the help and support of knowledgeable and sympathetic groups, the number of women suffering brutality at home will decrease. Through educational pathways it is hoped that fewer and fewer women will find themselves in violent relationships with men.

SOME NOTES ABOUT SEXUAL HARASSMENT

Sexual harassment is quite common. It takes place in practically every place of work. Almost 50 percent of all working women have been subjected to sexual harassment on the job.

Sexual harassment is a form of sex discrimination and is a crime forbidden under Title VII of the 1964 Civil Rights Act.

By definition set forth by the Equal Employment Opportunities Commission, the agency that enforces Title VII, sexual harassment is "Unwelcome sexual advances, requests for sexual favors, and other verbal and physical conduct of a sexual nature . . . when

- submission to such conduct is made a term or condition of an individual's employment,
- submission to or rejection of such conduct is used as the basis for promotional decision, or
- such conduct unreasonably interferes with work performance, or creates an intimidating, hostile or offensive working environment."

If a visitor or a nonsupervisory employee sexually harasses another employee, the employer is liable if he knows about the condition and fails to rectify it.

If a supervisor sexually harasses an employee, the employer is liable whether or not he knows. The supervisor is considered to be a representative of the employer.

Women in the Clergy

Beth Shalom Congregation in Clifton Park, New York, is a synagogue nestled in the seclusion of a rural area. For two years the synagogue had been without a rabbi until it accepted as its spiritual leader Rabbi Beverly Magidson. Although she has been ordained by the Reform Movement, Rabbi Magidson has not been accepted for membership in the Rabbinical Assembly, the governing body of the Conservative Movement. The congregation of Beth Shalom accepted a woman to fill their need for a full-time rabbi; a man would not have accepted the low pay offered by the 105-family synagogue. The congregation is very pleased with Rabbi Magidson's broad knowledge of Judaism and her ability to lead the congregation.

The Rev. Leslie Simonson is in the seventh year of her ministry at the Ridgeview Congregational Church (a member of the United Church of Christ) in White Plains, New York. Her husband serves with her as cominister. The

Rev. Leslie doesn't think that she would have obtained her position without being married to a minister. She credits her acceptance as a minister to the large number of professional women in her parish. In fact, she has noticed differences between her ministry and that of a male minister. In counseling, women parishioners seek her out because she can be more empathetic with problems facing women such as midlife crises, children leaving home, or money or health problems.

It is the exception rather than the rule for women to be accepted into the clergy by the Judaic or Christian faiths. The United Church of Christ, which never had a ban on women ministers, has 400 women ministers, the largest number in the United States. With a membership of 1.8 million, the United Church of Christ ranks seventh among the nation's denominations. Following is a summary of the number of women ministers in the predominant Protestant sects in the United States.

Denomination	Membership (Millions)	Number of Women Ministers
United Church of Christ	1.8	400
Disciples of Christ	1.3	388
United Methodist Church	9.9	319
United Presbyterian Church	2.6	295
Southern Baptist Convention	13.0	20

The Roman Catholic and the Greek Orthodox churches have not admitted women to the priesthood. The Church of England (Anglican) has an exclusively male priesthood; however, in others parts of the world the Anglican Church, with a membership of 65 million, has ordained 900 women as priests. The provinces of the Anglican Church include Hong Kong, Canada, New Zealand, Uganda, Kenya, and the Episcopal Church in the United States. In England, the General Synod, the church's council of bishops, clergy, and laity, has approved a plan to allow women to be ordained as deacons, which is the lowest rank of Anglican clergy. The Anglican Church in England and the Episcopal Church in the United States are investigating ways to give women a greater role in the policy-making of the church.

Similarly, the National Conference of Catholic Bishops has begun to focus on new roles for women in the Roman Catholic Church. James Malone, Bishop of Youngstown (Ohio), feels that particular attention must be given to women, that the role of laywomen and religious in church and in society must be clarified. He believes that their rights and dignity must be supported officially and that their advancement to positions of leadership and decision-making must be enhanced. Fulfilling a promise he had made, John Cardinal O'Connor has named a black woman vice chancellor of the Archdiocese of New York to assist the chancellor in his many administrative duties. This is the first time that a lay person and a woman has held that position in the New York Archdiocese.

The Protestant denominations are feeling an ever-increasing need for women clergy. Hundreds of small churches in many denominations are without pastors. Women clergy would be most useful in filling these voids and providing trained spiritual leadership for congregations that are without ministers. However, a climate of acceptance of women pastors has to be developed so that women of education with a call to the ministry can be used effectively to serve the needs of many who seek spiritual help.

Women in the Law

In the decades of the 1980s and '90s, more than 150,000 women have attended law school. Although not all persons who attend law school practice law, there are now many more women who earn their living as lawyers. However, some law firms still do not give women equal opportunity to become partners. Several suits are before the federal courts in which women lawyers have charged sex discrimination in the awarding of partnerships. Law firms expect partners to bring in business. The ability of women to do so cannot be measured by their limited history as partners. Law firms get their business from corporations. Since there are almost no women in the top ranks of corporations, it is not known whether women partners can attract corporation business.

Time changes situations. As more women enter the legal profession, the rank order of lawyers in law firms will change also. More women will probably have better opportunities for obtaining top jobs.

CHAPTER ◇ 7

Discrimination

Against Homosexuals

Each year tens of thousands of people march along New York City's Fifth Avenue on the last Sunday in June chanting, cheering, singing, and dancing in the annual Lesbian/Gay Pride Day Parade. The parade has been held since 1970 to commemorate the 1969 Stonewall Riots, which occurred after the police raided a bar frequented by homosexual men in Greenwich Village. Because the homosexual population of the city has woven itself into a vocal and politically active community, politicians regularly participate in the parade.

The parade represents the struggle by homosexuals for observance of the civil rights guaranteed by law. Gay people want the right to pursue their own life-style without discrimination or harassment. They want the full protection of the law and the right to live and work in their chosen endeavor without fear of persecution.

Backlash

Every time an oppressed group begins to petition for its civil rights, a backlash from some other group is provoked. Society is sometimes harsh toward male homosexuals. At various times their sexual behavior has been described as "crimes against nature." Although twenty-two states have repealed all laws against sexual behavior, the right to privacy has not been guaranteed by federal law. In March 1976 the United States Supreme Court upheld a lower court's decision that a state could prosecute and imprison people for homosexual activity, although conducted in private between consenting adults. The decision of the court was without doubt influenced by the "sodomy" statutes that remain in most states. Although rarely used except in cases of seduction of a minor, public indecency, or physical assault, the sodomy statutes serve as justification of legal harassment of male homosexuals.

In 1976 singer Anita Bryant initiated a drive against homosexuals that led to the 1977 repeal of the Dade County (Florida) homosexual rights ordinance. Her campaign seemed to stimulate violent acts against gay men by her supporters. Bumper stickers urging "Kill a Queer for Christ" were seen on cars. In various parts of the country, churches that welcomed homosexuals were vandalized. In St. Paul, Minnesota, in 1978, in response to a Baptist minister's campaign against homosexuals, the ordinance guaranteeing civil rights to gay people was reversed. A young homosexual gardener was stabbed to death by a youth gang who shouted "Faggot, faggot" as they brutally assaulted him.

Whenever there is forceful condemnation of an emotionally charged issue such as abortion or gay rights, people with unstable personalities are stimulated to carry out acts of violence. For example, public discussion of the abortion issue resulted in the bombing of abortion clinics by an unstable few. Public focus on homosexuality has led to abuses such as the raiding of a gay bar in Provincetown, Massachusetts (1977) and the arresting of seven gay men. The bar's liquor license was revoked but later reinstated by the State Alcoholic Beverage Control Commission.

A bar is a place where one makes social contacts among people of one's own liking. Just as there are "Irish" bars or "black" bars or "Italian" bars, so there are bars that cater to homosexuals. The law must guarantee that gay men can meet in places of public assembly without fear of arrest, assault, or harassment.

Homosexual Stereotypes

In Chapter 2 a stereotype was defined as a false mental picture that one group has of another. A stereotype is a powerful weapon of discrimination used to discredit a target group. Homosexuals are prime targets for stereotypes.

One such stereotype is that homosexual males are child molesters who prey on young boys. Many people believe that homosexuals must recruit young boys to their way of life or their pool of sex partners will be decreased. In truth, there is a signficant difference between a homosexual and a child molester: A homosexual is a person who prefers as a sex partner one of his or her own sex. Thus a homosexual male is attracted sexually to another male— not to a child.

A child molester is an adult who is driven by a compulsive attraction to children. A child molester may be heterosexual or homosexual. Statistics show that psychotic homsexuals who prey on young boys make up only 10 percent of the reported child molesters, and that 90 percent of reported child molesters are heterosexuals.

There is a myth that homosexuals are easily recognized. Some people think that all male homosexuals are effeminate and all female homosexuals masculine. That is not true. The Institute for Sex Research estimates that only 15 percent of male and 5 percent of female homosexuals are recognizable to most people. In physical appearance, homosexuals run the gamut of physiques and looks. Some lesbian women are very feminine. Gay men can look quite masculine, as did the late film star Rock Hudson and homosexual members of motorcycle gangs. Most gay men are quite average looking.

The Politics of Gay Rights

At the core of the gay rights movement is the struggle for the passing of legislation that will protect the civil rights of gay men and lesbians. Although most large cities have witnessed a greater acceptance of homosexual women and men in recent years, there is still the hard edge of resistance that prevents lawmakers from extending civil rights legislation to protect homosexuals. In New York, a city known for its liberal views, the City Council failed each year for fourteen years to pass a bill to protect homosexuals against discrimination. In 1986 such a law was passed after extraordinary public comment, pro and con.

The House of Delegates of the American Bar Association in 1985 defeated a resolution to press for federal legislation that would prohibit discrimination against homosexuals in housing, employment, and places of public accommodation. Although some 77 state, county, and local governments have passed such laws, the federal Civil Rights Act of 1964 does not cover homosexuals. That means that an estimated 25 million homosexuals do not have the full protection of federal law.

The opponents of legislation to bar discrimination against homosexuals reflect the type of prejudice that is bolstered by stereotyping. Many of the opposing delegates who were from the Southern and Southwestern states claimed that supporting the legislation would be an endorsement of homosexuality. However, the resolution stated clearly that the American Bar Association, "consistent with its longstanding opposition to unjust deprivation of civil rights and without approving or endorsing homosexual activity, urges the federal, state and local governments to adopt legislation barring discrimination based on sexual orientation."

Another argument against passing antidiscrimination legislation claimed it would mean that openly homosexual teachers could not be dismissed by public school boards. Interestingly, an Oklahoma law that empowered school boards to dismiss teachers for "advocating . . . encouraging or promoting public or private homosexual activity" was overturned by a federal appeals court. The State of Oklahoma has asked the Supreme Court for a review of the case.

The United Federation of Teachers and its parent organization, the American Federation of Teachers, and the National Education Association support the right of homosexuals to teach as long as they are professionally qualified. All advertisements for teachers prepared by the New York City Board of Education carry the slogan, "Equal Opportunity Employer—M/F/H." Yet many school boards outside of the city do fire teachers who openly admit homosexuality. However, in school districts where homosexuality is not an issue in hiring, there have been none of the negative consequences expected by those who oppose an open-hiring policy. According to a former president of the District of Columbia Board of Education, "Specifically, I know of no case in which our regulations have encouraged 'child recruitment' into homosexuality, 'child molestation' or proselytizing by our gay citizens toward young people that the homosexual lifestyle is a superior one . . . "

It is evident that persons involved in the drafting of laws must become cognizant of some basic facts regarding human sexuality. For example, a delegate opposed to civil rights legislation for homosexuals stated, " . . . This is not to be a question of unjust discrimination because it's not to punish somone for what they are, but for what they do. They don't have to be homosexuals." Such a statement makes it clear that the speaker does not know that no one has a choice in his or her sexuality, be it homosexuality, heterosexuality, or asexuality.

The American Psychological Association no longer considers homosexuality a result of pyschic disorders. Psychotherapists now help patients to accept their homosexual orientation without guilt and the stress that comes with it. Scientists have not been able to discover a genetic basis for homosexuality, nor a hormonal cause. Yet, unaccountably, a large segment of the population is so oriented. Most homosexuals assert that their sexuality is not a matter of choice, but a condition of life with which they must live.

Homosexuals and Organized Religion

In 1984 then Mayor Edward I. Koch of New York put into effect an executive order designed to protect homosexuals against job discrimination by agencies doing business with the city. The order forbade city contractors to hire employees on the basis of their "sexual orientation or affectional preference." Agencies doing business with the city were, in effect, to sign contracts that forbid job discrimination against homosexuals.

The city of New York pays more than 100 million dollars a year to Roman Catholic agencies, the Jewish Orthodox Agudath Israel of America, and the Salvation Army for acting as providers of child care. Of this total, the Catholic agencies receive about 76 million dollars. All three religious groups refused to sign a contract that would bar them from passing over homosexual applicants in hiring, each group claiming that such an order would be against their religious teachings.

The Salvation Army withdrew from the program and announced the closing of all its city-subsidized groups.

The more militant Archdiocese of New York under Cardinal O'Connor took the matter to court. The Appellate Division ruled in favor of the Mayor and his Executive Order 50. A few months later, however, the Court of Appeals overruled the decision of the Appellate Division. Executive Order 50 was declared null and void and could no longer be used to force the hiring of homosexuals by agencies that have contracts with the city.

The Roman Catholic Church is strong and unwavering in its opposition to homosexuality. However, the National Federation of Priests' Councils has openly supported measures that call for the civil rights of homosexuals. The Rev. John McNeil, a Jesuit priest, founded *Dignity*, an organization of Catholic gay men and lesbians. His open support of the homosexual community has caused him trouble with church officials. There is also an Episcopal group of homosexual lay people called *Integrity*, and gay organizations and synogogues for Jewish people.

In January 1977 the Episcopal Bishop of the Diocese of New York caused quite a stir by ordaining to the ministry an avowed lesbian. The act by Bishop Paul Moore, Jr. presented a double complication: not only was the candidate a lesbian, but also a *woman*. The Episcopal House of Bishops later voted against ordination for any "advocating or willful and habitual *practicing* homosexual" pending detailed study of the issue. It seemed that homosexual persons who are celibate might be acceptable for ordination.

The United Presbyterian Church at a Synod meeting in 1978 voted not to ordain homosexuals unless they were celibate and repentant. However, the Church strongly affirmed their civil and human rights.

The fundamentalist churches wage war against homosexuals. A certain fundamentalist preacher stated publicly that the disease AIDS is "retribution" for the sin of being homosexual. On the other hand, the National Council of Churches of Christ in the U.S.A. strongly supports the enacting of laws that grant full civil rights to homosexuals.

A Way of Coping: The Gay Subculture

Not admitted to the mainstream of society, all oppressed minorities find ways of coping with discrimination. One important method is avoiding the stress of rejection by establishing one's own subculture. Just as black Americans patronize their own barbers, hairdressers, and doctors and got to their own churches, so does the gay community patronize its own. Especially important for homosexual men are the services of homosexual doctors, who check them for oral and anal venereal disease. Gay men can get objective care from their own doctors without embarrassment. Gay people frequent certain resorts and gather at certain coffee houses, restaurants, bars, and beaches. They use their own travel agents and have formed their own churches. The Metropolitan Community Church was founded by Troy Perry for lesbians and gay men.

Another coping mechanism is the formation of organizations that work for gay rights and act on gay concerns. The National Gay Task Force and the Gay Rights Lobby work toward obtaining political rights for lesbians and gay men. Some very bright and talented people are activists in the gay community. They lend diligent efforts to help gays cope with their lives outside the mainstream of American society. They also try to educate the public about the contributions that gays can make to society at large. "Human beings of ability are rare. Some are homosexuals. We need them," said Henry G. Miller, who serves in the American Bar Association House of Delegates.

An important coping mechanism that has been developed on a sophisticated level in the gay community is networking. As AIDS (acquired immune deficiency syndrome) surfaced as an epidemic of death among the gay community, organizations such as the Gay Men's Health Crisis and the AIDS Resource Center, Inc. were formed immediately and developed support networks to meet the crisis. The services of lawyers, clergy, writers, physicians, research workers, entertainers, health care personnel, fund-raising lobbyists, volunteer workers, and people from all walks of life and with a variety of talents have been incorporated into this network, which aims to give comfort to those dying from AIDS, supply preventive methods to the well, and urge local, state, and federal governments to increase financial support to research the cause of the disease. Clinics have been established to help victims of AIDS, to give them counseling, to find them housing, and to attend to their needs in all practical ways. The Gay Men's Health Crisis has established a hot line that provides the latest information on the dread disease, which is now approaching the general population. Networking serves as a viable means of coping with conditions for which there may be no immediate solution.

"Homosexuals can aspire to anything any man can aspire to . . . they can be who they are . . . and achieve whatever their abilities allow them to do," says Criminal Court Judge Richard C. Failla, an open homosexual.

CHAPTER 8

The Handicapped: The Hidden Minority

Who Are the Handicapped?

A woman recounted to her church group the story of a little girl next door. When a new family moved in, three children were seen entering the house on moving day. As weeks wore on, only two of the children came out to play. When asked about their little sister, the two older children became mute and sullen and went in the house. Neighbors became suspicious, and the minister was asked to investigate discreetly. He found that the little girl who was kept out of sight was born with only one hand. The parents, feeling that this was God's punishment for some sin committed, hid the child from view. The minister urged the family to seek counseling after assuring them that this was an accident of birth and not punishment for sin.

The handicapped are people who have a physical or mental impairment that limits their function. A person might be lame, paralyzed, deaf, blind, or suffer from hemophilia or any other condition that limits functioning. A disabled person experiences daily difficulties and is deprived of commonplace experiences.

Just imagine not being able to get y wheelchair through a door or up the stairs, or not being able to hear a honking horn or ringing telephone. Not being able to see, or to control one's muscles, or even to sit upright unaided is a tough way to go through this world. Now we recognize that disabled persons do have great abilities that make the world richer if they are allowed to function in the mainstream and share their talents.

Some statistics about the population of the handicapped: 36 million people in the United States have physical or mental handicaps; one in six adults is handicapped; one in ten children has a handicapping disability; and one in three families has a handicapped member.

Let us take a minute to distinguish the meanings of some terms. A person who is *physically impaired* has a condition such as the loss of a limb or chronic muscle weakness or a health condition that makes him or her *physically disabled*—not able to walk or use arms or muscles or see or hear. The extent to which the disability limits the things the person can do is called a *handicap*. Although the terms physically impaired, physically disabled, and handicapped are used interchangeably, their meanings vary slightly.

A Changing View of the Disabled

When black Americans began demanding their civil rights in the 1960s, so did advocacy groups begin demanding civil rights for the handicapped. Chapter 4 discussed the release from mental institutions of large numbers of mentally impaired people at the urging of advocacy groups.

A physical impairment may not be totally handicapping (National Foundation March of Dimes).

Now many of these people live on the streets, constituting a new minority: the homeless. When one sees the conditions of their lives, one wonders if their civil rights were not violated by their release.

On the other hand, the rights of handicapped children to education was guaranteed by the enactment of Public Law 94–142. This law provides that all handicapped children, "the mentally retarded, hard of hearing, deaf, speech impaired, visually handicapped, severely emotionally disturbed, orthopedically handicapped, health impaired children or children with specific learning disabilities," are entitled to education at public expense. All school-age children who are handicapped must be given free and appropriate education according to the requirements of PL 94–102.

Public Law 03–112 forbids discrimination against the

handicapped of all ages. To meet its requirements, many places of business and industry have provided wheelchair-accessible ramps and elevators and have widened doorways.

The law has become very supportive of people who have experienced discrimination because of physical disability. Sometimes a physical characteristic may be perceived by another person as disabling. Such was the case for Catherine McDermott, who at 249 pounds was considered too obese to be hired by the Xerox Corporation as a systems analyst. For eleven years Mrs. McDermott (acting as her own lawyer) fought Xerox in court. A judge ruled in favor of Mrs. McDermott, saying that there was nothing in state law to "permit employers to refuse to hire persons who are able to do the job simply because they have a possibly treatable condition of excessive weight." The court ordered Xerox to hire Catherine McDermott with back pay and to take other remedial measures.

The Problems of the Disabled

We are beginning to take a closer look at the obstacles that prevent the handicapped from participating more fully in commonplace activities. The Architectural Barriers Act passed by Congress in 1968 requires that new buildings be made accessible to people with disabilities. Interior designers are devising ways to make homes barrier-free for those with physical handicaps.

Much has to be done to remove stereotypes about the handicapped. Many people believe that those who are disabled are ill, or mentally retarded, or lacking sex drives. The fact is that the disabled have the same dreams and aspirations as others. They resent being treated as second-class citizens and want to be part of the mainstream of life. Psychologists find that stereotypes are most easily eradicated when the able-bodied public has more contact with the disabled. Education and open-mindedness are the pathways to attitude changes.

A major problem is helping the disabled to become functional in the world of work. On one hand, government assistance maintains the disabled at the poverty level. Very little has been done to train the physically handicapped to do jobs of which they are capable. Part of the problem is transportation to work and accessibility of the workplace. In some cities buses have lifts to accommodate people in wheelchairs. Some transit systems have both light and audio signals.

The Rehabilitation Act of 1973 prohibits job discrimination against disabled persons; however, the law cannot be enforced if the disability does not allow the person to function at the job. Many companies are making efforts to accommodate wheelchair-bound persons, deaf people, and even the blind. An organization called The Job Accommodation Network at the University of West Virginia has compiled 4,000 ideas to help companies accommodate the disabled, among them how deaf people can use the telephone and how desks can be designed to permit use by people in wheelchairs.

Personal Despondency

People who work with the handicapped know of their personal struggles to become part of the world in which they live. It is hard to adjust to disability and takes unusual effort to do so. The attitudes of other people affect the way a handicapped person thinks of himself. Many handicapped persons suffer from low self-esteem because of the indifference and rejection of others and thus do not aspire to attain goals. Low self-esteem also contributes to the pattern of living in isolation that is accepted by so many of the handicapped.

Education seems to be the key in making disabled persons acceptable to themselves and to others. As handicapped children are put into classes with the general school population, they become a natural part of the classroom society. As children mature, both the able and the disabled, the acceptance of persons with physical disabilities becomes natural. Disabled people need love and support, which can be generated by the people with whom they have contact and by the influence of the mass media. A handicapping condition is not easy to live with. All of us must make every effort to involve the handicapped in the mainstream of life.

CHAPTER ◊ 9

Coping as a Way
of Doing

C oping means action. When people cope with a
problem, they meet it head on, struggle with it,
and find the means to deal with it. Discrimination
against black Americans, Jews, disabled persons, native
Americans, Asians, immigrants, homosexuals, the homeless, and the countless others in target populations is an
intolerable denial of human rights to a large segment of
our population. The civil rights movement during the
1960s showed us that many Americans were denied the
right to function in the mainstream of life because of discriminatory laws and practices. When laws exist that
militate against an ethnic, racial, or religious group, what
forces can be brought to bear to remove those laws?

Legal Remedies

The Civil Rights Act of 1964 declared that "separate" was
not equal, never was equal, and cannot be equal. Charles

The late Dr. Martin Luther King, Jr., who began the Civil Rights
Movement in the United States by organizing bus boycotts in
Montgomery, Ala. (Schomburg Center for Research in Black Culture,
The New York Public Library, Astor, Lenox and Tilden Foundations).

Johnson, a civil rights lawyer who practices in Pasadena,
California, worked actively in the civil rights movement.
He maintains that the remedy against discrimination is
the astute use of the legal process. The trick is to apply
the remedy effectively so that it can work against the
disease.

The precursor to the remedy is developing a public mind-set that will react favorably to the changes sought. Martin Luther King provided perceptive and compelling leadership. Through his brilliant oratory he identified the problems that denied human rights to black Americans and thus raised public consciousness. His view was not myopic. Not only did he work on behalf of black Americans, but also for all oppressed people regardless of race, religion, or national origin. Dr. King worked tirelessly for civil rights and wisely chose the course of *nonviolent* confrontation. For his work, Dr. King was awarded the Nobel Peace Prize.

Much of the remedy against discrimination is in the law, but it must be used wisely. Thurgood Marshall, an expert in constitutional law and the chief lawyer of the National Association for the Advancement of Colored People, started the pot of desegregation boiling in 1954. It was then that he challenged in the Supreme Court the legality of segregated schools in the South. The winning of this landmark case was the beginning of the end of segregation supported by law in American courts of justice.

Education as a Remedy

Education is the ladder of upward movement: intellectual, economic, and social. In segregated societies, schooling and quality schools are always denied to those groups against whom the system is working. This was true of the segregated South in the U.S. as it is currently true under the apartheid system in South Africa. Lack of education robs one of initiative and limits effective response.

Recently a document was promulgated by the Vatican that called for an end to the presenting of Judaism in a "prejudiced, distorted manner" and urged study to

The remedy: better education and political awareness has enabled native Americans to demand civil rights (Association on American Indian Affairs).

"help in understanding the meaning for the Jews of the Holocaust." However, leaders of Jewish organizations found the document inadequate in its presentation of the impact of the Holocaust or the creation of Israel. Through the efforts of educated Catholics and Jews a more acceptable document was to be worked out to remove the "deeply troublesome references" that were regarded as regressive by Jewish organizations.

Asian-Americans are currently questioning the admissions policies of Ivy League colleges. About 70 to 75 percent of the Asian-Americans who apply to college are premedical students or in other areas of science or mathematics. Other minority groups apply in much smaller numbers. For example, more than twice as many Asian-Americans as blacks apply to Princeton although there are five times as many blacks in the United States. The Asian-Americans do not fall into any special preference group such as children of alumni or athletes. Therefore the choice in admissions seems to be between Asian-Americans who come from the suburbs and have an excellent command of English and those from the city who are superior in the sciences but lack skill in the language. To resolve this problem, several Ivy League colleges employ Asian-American recruiters and admission officers to reduce the bias that otherwise might influence admission of Asian-Americans.

Unlike the public protests of the 1960s by which black Americans called attention to injustices, the Asian-Americans prefer to work within the system through university committees. However, some feel that because they are so low-key, colleges overlook their requests for Asian-American admissions data. The younger generation have become more persistent in their demands for fairer policies. As one person put it, "Protest, even quiet protest, is a sign of Americanization."

Education has made the difference between the black middle class and the uneducated underclass. Blacks have become increasingly visible in almost every facet of

American life, from sports to politics to business to enter-
tainment. The Bill Cosby television show about a middle-
class black family has triumphed in ratings. The show is
not a "black" show; it is merely a situation comedy that
could take place in any family, and it indicates that there is
a refocusing of social issues among Americans in general.
The black American college student and graduate are more
interested in financial success and becoming prosperous
entrepreneurs. Blacks are striving to gain a firm footing in
the economy and in the political arena. A special issue of
Ebony Magazine, "Blacks and the Future: Where Will
We Be in the Year 2000?" (August, 1985), provided an
excellent summary of the progress of black Americans and
encouraging predictions about their progress in all fields
of endeavor.

Most of America's half million or more West Indian
immigrants have settled in Brooklyn, New York. The West
Indians are black, but prosperous. The question is often
asked: If racism is such a crushing burden on blacks, why
have the West Indians done so well? Economist Thomas
Sowell believes that out of West Indian slavery "emerged
a more self-reliant, independent and defiant population
than emerged out of U.S. slavery." Whatever the reason,
West Indians, like other immigrant groups, work very
hard to achieve. A great percentage of them work two
and even three low-paying jobs. They save money, buy
houses, and shun welfare assistance. According to former
Congresswoman Shirley Chisholm. "There are two things
every West Indian wants to get when he arrives here, an
education and a house." Unlike the ghetto neighborhoods,
the West Indian areas are well kept. It has been said that
the householder is like a stake holder; he is like a small
farmer rather than a tenant farmer.

The Remedy of Economics

The apartheid system in South Africa is abhorrent to all who believe in the dignity of the human being. Fifty-two companies have formed the U.S. Corporate Council on South Africa, which, with 160 more companies, has called for reforms:

- An end to racial discrimination in the workplace;
- Equal and fair employment practices;
- Equal pay for equal or comparable work;
- Training programs to prepare blacks and nonwhites for supervisory and administrative jobs;
- An increase in the number of blacks and nonwhites in management and supervisory jobs;
- Improvement in the quality of employees' lives in such areas as housing and education.

The Council is playing an active role in ending apartheid in South Africa and supports South African businessmen who promise to work toward that goal. Segregation in our own Southern states was a barrier to economic and industrial expansion. In South Africa, an end to apartheid will come when the pressure from business intensifies.

Coping with discrimination requires effort and commitment. The commitment by the individual must involve seeking education and developing marketable skills. Group effort requires political action and working through the legal process to eradicate laws that do not serve the cause of justice.

CHAPTER 10

Changing Ways

The civil rights activities of the 1960s did not wither away at the end of that decade. Instead, the civil rights movement has blossomed into a lasting consciousness of human rights. The idea that all people are entitled to equal protection under the law has become part of the mind-set of people throughout the world.

The civil rights activities of the '60s served to identify the social, economic, and educational injustices that denied human rights to black Americans. The "white only" signs, segregated seating in public places, segregated schools, and denial of jobs and economic opportunity were not hidden. In fact, laws enforced those discriminatory practices. Therefore, it required legal processes to do away with them.

As the injustices inflicted on black people were brought to light, other groups of Americans began to identify acts of discrimination against themselves. Continuing in the decade of the 1990s is the legacy of human rights awareness begun three decades ago. Laws continue to be refined and reshaped to change situations that discriminate against people.

Women's Health Research Issues

Medical scientists learn about the causes and signs of disease through research. The National Institutes of Health (NIH) are research agencies sponsored by the United States government. It is the responsibility of the NIH to study the health of *all* people.

The General Accounting Office, the investigative agency of Congress, has charged that the NIH does not include women in its clinical studies. In a study on the effect of aspirin in reducing heart attack, a panel of 22,000 men was used. Not one woman was included. Further, in a study to identify risk factors for heart disease not one woman was included among 15,000 men used. The largest study ever done on aging was carried out over a twenty-year period (1958–1978). That study also excluded women.

The Congressional Caucus for Women's Issues is a watchdog group composed of women in Congress. Representatives Patricia Schroeder (D-Colorado) and Olympia J. Snowe (R-Maine) introduced a bill in Congress called the Women's Health Equity Act. The bill calls for establishment of a center for women's health research at NIH. Senator Barbara A. Mikulski (D-Maryland) has stated that less than 14 percent of the NIH budget for research is spent on women's health projects.

Medical scientists know that female physiology differs from the male. For example, a woman's liver breaks down cholesterol in a process different from that of a man. No research has been done to find out why this is so. Excluding women from health research studies works against the health of all women and is a glaring form of discrimination.

Women in the Workplace

Discrimination in the workplace is an ongoing problem for women. Workplace discrimination may take the form of denial of hiring in certain types of jobs, denial of promotion to top-level jobs, or sexual harassment. When discrimination is subtle (hidden), it is hard to prove and therefore difficult to correct. A case in point is the role of women in unions.

The A.F.L.-C.I.O now has 17.1 million members. Women, who are joining unions at a higher rate than men, make up one out of three members. However, only three women sit on the Executive Council of 315 members. The A.F.L.-C.I.O. gives only lip service to issues of women's rights and racial equality. In fact, the internal structure of the union does not support social change.

Jobs that have been traditionally all male are being opened up to females. The first women who choose to break the sex barrier in the workplace are usually exposed to harassment. How long the harassment continues depends on the strength of the policy of equity in a particular work situation. The National Football League recently fined a coach $30,000 for excluding a woman reporter from his team's locker room. Two women who became sanitation workers were not so well protected from demeaning remarks by their male coworkers.

Women in the legal profession are using the law to help fight discriminatory practices. Two female attorneys won a class action suit for 150 women against the Missouri Highway and Transportation Commission. Women had been denied maintenance jobs on the basis of sex. An entry-level maintenance job required an eighth-grade education and ability to operate lightweight motor equipment such as pickup trucks, tractors, and mowers. A federal judge awarded the women more than $2.2 million in damages.

Sexual Harassment

What exactly is meant by sexual harassment? In general, a person is harassed when a single person or a group continuously behave in an ugly, threatening way to her or him. Federal law defines sexual harassment as offensive teasing, demeaning jokes, threatening gestures, unwanted physical contact, or explicit sexual advances.

Many law firms are establishing antiharassment codes to protect professional women from distasteful behavior by partners, associates, and other males. A lawyer at the Securities and Exchange Commission who was denied promotion because she refused sexual advances by a partner was awarded back pay and promotion.

Of the two million people who are on active duty in the military, women make up 11 percent. A recent survey by the Defense Department revealed that a third of women military personnel had been subjected to sexual harassment. Persons who commit such offenses receive stiff penalties. Defense Department support has decreased incidents of sexual harassment in the military.

Equal Pay for Equal Work

A current struggle for professional women is obtaining the pay scale given to men for the same work. Women research scientists are usually paid less than men. Law firms tend to pay female associates less. Recently the federal Equal Employment Opportunity Commission ruled in favor of a television anchorwoman. Her male counterparts received salaries of $180,000 per year, whereas she received only

$140,000. The TV station was ordered to increase her pay to equal that of the anchormen.

Grievances about lower pay for women are settled through the legal process when there are laws that cover the job situation. Research scientists work per research project and the pay is set by the laboratory director, by a governing board, or by a fee set in a grant. Somehow women scientists receive lower pay, and the situation is not currently governed by legal guidelines. It can be expected that a way to establish pay equity in research laboratories will be devised.

Issues of Gay Rights

Sodomy is not a word that one hears in everyday conversation. Sodomy refers to sexual relationships between men. (It also refers to certain heterosexual practices). Before 1961 all states had sodomy laws, meaning that homosexuality was a crime. During the past three decades most states have repealed their sodomy laws.

Advocates of civil rights and personal freedoms have sought to have sodomy laws removed from the books in every state. The Supreme Court of the United States has to refused to rule on sodomy laws, stating that the Constitution does not protect homosexual activity.

Sixteen states plus the District of Columbia still have sodomy laws that ban homosexual activity: Alabama, Arizona, Connecticut, Georgia, Idaho, Louisiana, Maryland, Massachusetts, Minnesota, Mississippi, North Carolina, Oklahoma, Rhode Island, South Carolina, Utah, Virginia. In an effort to eliminate those laws civil rights interest groups are seeking help through state courts. A state court in Texas has removed sodomy laws from the books.

Lesbians and Political Office

Lesbian women and gay men have learned to work together to solve common problems. At one time they were at odds, vying for political leadership, but the AIDS epidemic healed the rift. When AIDS began to destroy the gay male population, lesbian women assumed leadership in the struggle against the disease by organizing fundraising campaigns and establishing health-care clinics. Their leadership role has continued into politics.

In November 1990 five out of six acknowledged lesbians were elected to public office throughout the country. In New York City, Deborah Glick became the first openly gay person elected to the New York State Assembly. She was strongly supported by the gay community.

Changing Education for Minorities

The honorary chairwoman of the State Council on Children and Families is Matilda R. Cuomo, wife of New York Governor Mario Cuomo. Through the Council Mrs. Cuomo helped establish a mentoring program in the Albany elementary schools. She makes regular visits to the home and school of the youngster whom she mentors, checking the child's study habits and school progress and assisting the family in special matters. Mentoring establishes a positive relationship between a child from a needy family and a knowledgeable adult. The mentor helps the child to develop positive feelings about school and thus make greater progress.

Helping to Change Attitudes

Educators and community workers have identified attitudes that prevent minority youngsters from doing well in school. First, many minority young people do not feel good about themselves. They do not have a feeling of well-being. When people hurt inside and feel bad about themselves, we say that they lack self-esteem, which prevents them from achieving. Also contributing to below-standard school achievement are negative peer pressure and the ideology of inner-city streets. Drug abuse, idleness, and crime steer minority young people away from the educational system and into the criminal justice system. Third, parental ignorance about the benefits to be gained from education discourages young people from participating as they should in the classroom.

To change the self-defeating attitudes of minority youth, a number of uplift programs have been started by interested organizations and individuals. Mayor David Dinkins of New York City has started a year-round employment and education program for poor and minority young people. The goal of the program is to encourage youngsters to remain in school. As they improve academically, they also learn work skills and earn money, receiving stipends for tutoring and for work experience.

A growing number of Sunday afternoon conferences are being held for black youths. The purpose is to urge the black male to remain in school. The black educators and community people who run the conferences discuss not only the value of education but also the hard issues of life on inner-city streets. Much emphasis is placed on the soaring homicide rate among young black males, black-on-black crime, and the state of the black family. Conference leaders hope to change attitudes into those that will work for the benefit of minority youth.

Schools Can Work

Boys and Girls High School in the Bedford-Stuyvesant section of Brooklyn has become the focus of national attention. Principal Frank Mickens has turned a volatile and underachieving school into a safe and stable place where students are achieving. One of his first acts as principal was to enlist the aid of the community to remove drug-dealing youths from the school. Once that was accomplished, the school could be improved in other ways.

With strong support from the parent and student council, Principal Mickens banned the wearing of gold jewelry and tooth caps and expensive leather jackets. In the inner cities, young people are robbed of attractive property by criminal gangs. Some youngsters lose their lives trying to protect their valuables. Mickens has also established a male dress code requiring the wearing of dress shirts and ties.

Pupils at Boys and Girls High School have responded positively to the changing ways of the school. Because the environment is now stable, calm, and safe, the teaching staff can teach and pupils can learn.

School for Minority Males

To build self-esteem and responsible behavior in black males, the city of Milwaukee is undertaking a somewhat controversial program. Two schools, an elementary school and a middle school, are to be set up exclusively for African-American males. The purpose is to provide the traditional academic curriculum and also courses emphasizing African-American culture and history.

The New York City Board of Education is planning a pilot school that would put special emphasis on the problems of black and Hispanic males. To be called the Ujamaa Institute (*ujamaa* is the Swahili word for "family"), the school will stress family life and values. A school exclusively for black and Hispanic males presents problems of race and sex discrimination, which will have to be worked out.

Changing Ideas Change Ways

A number of discriminatory practices have been corrected through the legal process. Laws supporting discrimination have been overturned and replaced with laws that grant human rights. Once in a while a rash of racist incidents occur on college campuses. Through the use of special seminars and restructuring of rules, college administrators have addressed these incidents.

Changing ideas have changed ways of thinking about what makes a practice discriminatory. Until recently women beaten by their husbands or male companions were not protected by law. The new breed of women in the legal profession have taken up the cause of their battered sisters. For example, attorneys Marjory Fields, Elyse Lehman, and Ellen Levine have written the *Handbook for Beaten Women*, which provides step-by-step directions on how battered women can protect themselves and get legal help. Social service agencies have established shelters for battered women.

The then Governor of Ohio, Richard F. Celeste, in 1990 granted pardons to 25 women who had been convicted of killing or assaulting husbands or male companions who had physically abused them over a long period of time. The Governor used powers the law granted him to correct legal injustice.

Changing Ways and Future Solutions

New ways of looking at old problems have helped to change some discriminatory laws and practices. As laws change, so does the thinking of people. The enactment of the Civil Rights Act of 1964 brought a number of changes in thinking about discrimination. Affirmative action programs were devised to help minority men and women obtain jobs and get into schools that were previously closed to them. Now in the decade of the '90s, affirmative action programs are being reexamined. That is the American process: reexamination and then orderly change through law. Not all discriminatory practices have been done away with. Future answers to coping with discrimination will arise from ongoing concerns.

Appendix A

**HOW TO FILE A COMPLAINT ABOUT
VIOLATION OF CIVIL RIGHTS**

Your written complaint should include the following
information:

Your name
Your address including zip code
The name and address of the person the complaint is
against
A complete description of the discrimination, with the
date or dates, place or places, and names of persons
who can help describe or support your complaint

If you are in doubt as to which agency you should
contact, send your complaint to:

Office of General Counsel
U.S. Commission on Civil Rights
Washington, DC 20425

WHERE TO FILE A COMPLAINT

Discrimination in:	*Write to:*
Voting	Assistant Attorney General Civil Rights Division U.S. Department of Justice Washington, DC 20530
Public accommodations	Same as above
Government-owned or -operated facilities	Same as above
Police brutality or lack of police protection	Same as above
Public schools and colleges	Director, Office of Civil Rights U.S. Department of Education Washington, DC 20201
Farm programs	Assistant to the Secretary for Civil Rights Department of Agriculture Washington, DC 20250
Antipoverty programs	Assistant Director for Civil Rights Office of Economic Opportunity Washington, DC 20506
Employment in private sector	Assistant Attorney General Civil Rights Division U.S. Department of Justice Washington, DC 20530
Employment by a company having federal contracts	Director Office of Federal Contract Compliance Washington, DC 20210
State employment programs	Coordinator of Civil Rights Activities Department of Labor Washington, DC 20210
Employment by the federal government	Board of Appeals and Review U.S. Civil Service Commission Washington, DC 20415

ORGANIZATIONS THAT WORK AGAINST HATE GROUPS

Southern Law Poverty Center
Klanwatch Project
400 Washington Avenue, P.O. Box 548
Montgomery, AL 36195-5101

National Anti-Klan Network
P.O. Box 10500
Atlanta, GA 30310

Anti-Defamation League of B'nai B'rith
Offices nationwide; consult telephone book

National Institute Against Prejudice and Violence
525 West Redwood Street
Baltimore, MD 21201

Institute for Research and Education on
   Human Rights, Inc.
P.O. Box 6001
Kansas City, MO 64110

Appendix B

PREJUDICE SURVEY

Psychologists tell us that prejudice is learned from people whom we we admire and respect.

- Do you have any prejudices? If so, what are they?
- Do members of your family have any prejudices? If so, what are they?
- Do your close friends have any prejudices? If so, what are they?

Prejudice may occur when people experience hard times, such as job loss.

- Can you identify such a prejudice and trace it back to its origin?
- Is there any reliable way that you can refute such a prejudice?

Prejudice may occur if a person has a bad experience with a member of another group. The bad experience is then generalized to the whole group.

- Can you identify such a prejudice and trace it back to its origin?
- How may a person cope with an unpleasant experience without resorting to prejudice?

Psychologists tell us that very prejudiced people are those who have a very poor self-image.

- Do you know a very prejudiced person? If so, describe his (her) personality.
- How can you change the mind of a prejudiced person?
- Have the person's prejudices been helpful to himself or to others? If so, how?
- Is there any way that you might help to improve a person's self-image?

Sometimes one person hates another on first sight.

- Did you ever take an instant dislike to a person? If so, why?
- After you got to know the person, did you change your mind?
- How can you find out what a person is really like?
- Have you ever had prejudice directed at you? If so, how did you cope?
- Is prejudice a part of human nature? Cite reasons for your answer.

DETECTING SEX AND RACE BIAS IN DAILY SPEECH

Can you find bias in the statements that follow? If so, classify the type.

	Sex Bias	Race Bias	No Bias
1. Joseph was the black sheep of his family.	___	___	___
2. Eileen Ferguson is a successful woman lawyer.	___	___	___

3. The police officers were quite helpful.   ——   ——   ——

4. The Chief Executive met with the well-dressed black officials.   ——   ——   ——

5. The purpose of advertising is to reach the "common man."   ——   ——   ——

6. The teacher asked a strong boy to carry the books.   ——   ——   ——

7. Mrs. Thompson warned her children against acting like wild Indians.   ——   ——   ——

8. Basketball is a tall person's game.   ——   ——   ——

9. Mailmen are expected to work in all kinds of weather.   ——   ——   ——

10. The Pilgrims brought their wives to the New World with them.   ——   ——   ——

11. Women have trouble balancing their checkbooks.   ——   ——   ——

12. Mary Carter is considered an attractive professor. Her husband is a brilliant mathematician.   ——   ——   ——

13. "Of course you can do math," said the counselor. "All Chinese are good in math."   ——   ——   ——

14. The high cabinets were suitable for a tall man.   ——   ——   ——

15. Good athletes take their training seriously.   ——   ——   ——

Bibliography

Aran, Kenneth, et al. *The History of Black Americans.* UFT, New York, 1972.

Bauer, Yehuda. *A History of the Holocaust.* Franklin Watts, New York, 1982.

Becker, Evelyn, et al. *Topics in Jewish American Heritage.* UTT, New York, 1975.

Cross, Theodore. *The Black Power Imperative.* Faulkner Books, New York, 1987.

Deloria, Jr., Vine. *Behind the Trail of Broken Treaties.* Delacorte Press, New York, 1974.

————. *We Talk You Listen.* Macmillan, New York, 1970.

————. *Indians of the Pacific Northwest.* Doubleday, New York, 1977.

Korman, Gerd, et al. *Hunter and Hunted: History of the Holocaust.* B'nai B'rith, 1973.

McCarthy, Joe, *Ireland.* Life World Library, New York, 1964.

————. *South Africa.* Life World Library, 1964.

Thayer, Charles W. *Russia.* Life World Library, New York, 1960.

Whittemore, L.H. *Together.* William Morrow Co., New York, 1971

Wilkinson, J. Harve. *From Brown to Bakke.* Oxford University Press, New York, 1979.

Index